AI-Powered Real Estate: 2024's Guide to Automated Deal Finding

Harness Cutting-Edge Tech to Uncover Market Treasures

By

Ernie Braveboy

Foreword

In the rapidly evolving landscape of the 21st century, where technology and innovation continually redefine the boundaries of possibility, the domain of real estate stands as a prime example of this transformative wave. "AI and Real Estate: Mastering Automated Investments in 2024" by Ernie Braveboy is a seminal work that delves deep into the heart of this revolution, offering a comprehensive guide to navigating the uncharted territories of tech-enabled real estate investments.

As we stand on the brink of 2024, the fusion of artificial intelligence and real estate investment strategies heralds a new era of opportunity and challenge. This book emerges as an essential beacon for professionals, investors, and enthusiasts alike, aiming to demystify the complexities of AI-driven methodologies in the real estate sector. Ernie Braveboy, with his astute insights and practical wisdom, guides readers through the intricacies of leveraging technology to enhance decision-making processes, optimize investment outcomes, and foresee market trends with unprecedented accuracy.

"AI and Real Estate" is not merely a technical manual but a visionary exploration of the future. It challenges conventional paradigms and encourages a proactive embrace of innovation, positioning readers at the forefront of an industry undergoing profound transformation. Through a carefully curated blend of case studies, theoretical frameworks, and real-world applications, the author elucidates the pivotal role of AI in scouting, analyzing, and securing real estate deals that were once beyond the grasp of traditional methodologies.

This book is a clarion call to action for those poised to lead in the digital age of real estate. It equips its readers with the knowledge, tools, and confidence to venture into the frontier of tech-enabled deal hunting, where the synergy of human insight and artificial intelligence paves the way for unprecedented achievements.

As you turn the pages of "AI and Real Estate: Mastering Automated Investments in 2024," prepare to embark on an enlightening journey through the evolving landscapes of technology and real estate. Under the guidance of Ernie Braveboy, embrace the future with an informed perspective and an unwavering resolve to master the art and science of automated investments in the dynamic world of 2024 and beyond.

Welcome to the frontier of real estate investment – where the future is not just imagined but built, one intelligent decision at a time.

Ernie Braveboy invites you to step into the future with him, exploring the vast potential of AI in transforming real estate investments. May this book serve as your compass in the exciting journey ahead.

Table of Contents

1. INTRODUCTION 1
    UNDERSTANDING AI IN REAL ESTATE 2
    PURPOSE OF THIS GUIDE 5
2. BASICS OF AI IN REAL ESTATE 7
    WHAT IS AI AND HOW DOES IT WORK? 9
    THE ROLE OF AI IN REAL ESTATE 12
3. STARTING WITH AI: WHAT YOU NEED TO KNOW 15
    KEY AI CONCEPTS FOR REAL ESTATE INVESTORS 18
    UNDERSTANDING DATA: THE FOUNDATION OF AI 21
4. AI TOOLS FOR FINDING REAL ESTATE DEALS 25
    OVERVIEW OF AI TOOLS AND PLATFORMS 29
    HOW AI IDENTIFIES POTENTIAL DEALS 33
5. USING AI TO ANALYZE MARKET TRENDS 37
    PREDICTIVE ANALYTICS FOR REAL ESTATE 40
    CASE STUDIES: AI PREDICTING MARKET SHIFTS 44
6. AI IN PROPERTY VALUATION 48
    AUTOMATED VALUATION MODELS (AVMS) 51
    ACCURACY AND RELIABILITY OF AI VALUATIONS 55
7. AI FOR DUE DILIGENCE IN REAL ESTATE 59
    STREAMLINING PROPERTY RESEARCH WITH AI 63
    AI IN ASSESSING PROPERTY CONDITIONS 66
8. FINDING OFF-MARKET PROPERTIES WITH AI 71
    TECHNIQUES FOR UNCOVERING HIDDEN GEMS IN REAL ESTATE 74
    SUCCESS STORIES: AI AND OFF-MARKET DEALS 79
9. THE FUTURE OF AI IN DEAL-FINDING 83
    UPCOMING TRENDS IN AI AND REAL ESTATE 86
    WHAT NEXT FOR INVESTORS IN THE AI-ENHANCED REAL ESTATE LANDSCAPE? ..89
10. IMPLEMENTING AI IN YOUR INVESTMENT STRATEGY 93
    GETTING STARTED WITH AI TOOLS IN REAL ESTATE 96

BEST PRACTICES FOR AI INTEGRATION IN REAL ESTATE......................................99

11. CONCLUSION: NAVIGATING THE FUTURE OF REAL ESTATE WITH AI 103

RECAP OF KEY INSIGHTS FROM "NAVIGATING THE FUTURE OF REAL ESTATE WITH AI" 106

1. Introduction

In the electrifying realm of real estate, a revolution is underway, and at its heart lies the pulsating power of artificial intelligence. "The Future of Property Investment: AI Strategies for 2024" is not just a guide; it's your gateway to the untapped potential of AI in unearthing the hidden treasures of the property market. As a best-selling author, I've traversed the landscapes of innovation and investment, and now, I'm here to take you on a journey where technology meets tenacity, transforming the way we perceive, pursue, and procure real estate investments.

This book is a beacon for those ready to sail the vast oceans of the property market, armed with the most advanced technological compass—AI. Whether you're charting your first course in real estate or you're a seasoned navigator of property investments, the insights within these pages are designed to illuminate your path with the brilliance of AI-driven strategies.

The fusion of AI and real estate is not just a fleeting trend; it's the dawn of a new era where data becomes your most trusted advisor, and intuition meets information. We'll delve deep into the essence of AI, peeling back the layers to reveal how machine learning, natural language processing, and geographic information systems are not just tools but allies in your quest for the most lucrative deals.

Through the tapestry of real-world success stories, we'll explore the triumphs and trials of those who've harnessed AI to turn the tides in their favor. These narratives are not just stories; they're blueprints of innovation, resilience, and foresight. And as we peer into the crystal ball of technology, we'll uncover the emerging trends that promise to redefine the boundaries of real estate investment.

But this book is more than just a collection of insights and foresights; it's a clarion call to action. It's an invitation to join the vanguard of investors who are not just witnessing the future but are actively shaping it with every decision, every deal, and every daring leap into the AI-enhanced realm of property investment.

So, embark with me on this thrilling expedition into the heart of the AI revolution in real estate. Let "The Future of Property Investment: AI Strategies for 2024" be your map to the treasures that lie hidden, just waiting to be discovered by those bold enough to look beyond the horizon and seize the future today.

Understanding AI in Real Estate

In the ever-evolving narrative of real estate, a new chapter is being written by the hands of Artificial Intelligence (AI). This technology, once the realm of science fiction, has now become a pivotal player in the property market, offering a lens through which we can view and understand the complexities of real estate in a new light. This chapter aims to unravel the enigma of AI, making it accessible and relatable to you, whether you're a novice dipping your toes into the property pool or a seasoned investor navigating the currents of the market.

The Essence of AI in Real Estate

At its core, AI is about the replication of human intelligence processes by machines, particularly computer systems. These processes encompass learning, which involves acquiring information and the rules for its use; reasoning, which refers to using the acquired information to reach conclusions; and self-correction, which focuses on improving over time. In the realm of real estate, AI taps into vast datasets to identify patterns, predict outcomes, and provide insights that were previously beyond our grasp.

Pillars of AI in Property Investment

1. **Machine Learning:** Imagine a system that not only learns from past data but also adapts its predictions and suggestions based on new information. Machine learning algorithms in real estate sift through historical property data, analyze current market conditions, and even keep tabs on emerging trends to spot potential investment opportunities and predict property value trends.

2. **Natural Language Processing (NLP):** This technology enables computers to understand human language as it is spoken or written. In real estate, NLP is used to analyze listings, client inquiries, and market news, extracting meaningful insights about property features, investor sentiment, and market movements.

3. **Predictive Analytics:** By leveraging historical data, statistical algorithms, and machine learning techniques, predictive analytics can forecast future market trends, property values, and investment risks. This allows

investors to make data-driven decisions, reducing uncertainty and maximizing returns.

4. **Geospatial Analysis:** With Geographic Information Systems (GIS), AI analyzes data with geographical components, offering insights into location trends, neighborhood development, and the spatial relationships between key real estate factors.

Transformative Impact of AI on Real Estate

The introduction of AI into the real estate sector has led to significant advancements in how properties are discovered, evaluated, and traded. Here's a glimpse into the transformative effects of AI:

- **Enhanced Property Discovery:** AI-powered platforms provide personalized property recommendations by analyzing investors' preferences, investment history, and market trends, streamlining the property search process.
- **Accurate Valuation Models:** AI algorithms assess a multitude of factors affecting property prices, offering real-time valuations that aid investors in making informed decisions quickly.
- **Risk Assessment:** AI's ability to analyze historical data and current market conditions helps identify potential investment risks, allowing for more strategic decision-making.
- **Investment Portfolio Optimization:** AI can pinpoint the most promising investment opportunities based on specific criteria, such as yield, location, and risk, assisting in the creation of a diversified and optimized portfolio.

As we delve deeper into the intersection of AI and real estate, it becomes clear that AI is not merely a tool but a game-changer, offering new perspectives and opportunities in property investment. Understanding and leveraging AI can empower investors to navigate the market with greater insight, efficiency, and success.

Purpose of This Guide

The purpose of this guide, "The Future of Property Investment: AI Strategies for 2024," is multifaceted, designed to serve as a beacon for those navigating the complex, rapidly evolving intersection of artificial intelligence and real estate investment. This guide aims to:

1. **Demystify Artificial Intelligence:** By breaking down complex AI concepts into understandable segments, this guide seeks to demystify the technology for a broad audience. It aims to clarify how AI functions within the realm of real estate, making advanced technologies accessible to all levels of investors.
2. **Showcase AI's Transformative Power:** Through detailed exploration, the guide illuminates the transformative potential of AI in revolutionizing property investment. It highlights how AI can enhance decision-making processes, uncover hidden market opportunities, and optimize investment strategies.
3. **Provide Practical Insights and Strategies:** This guide is not just theoretical; it offers practical insights and actionable strategies. It aims to equip investors with the knowledge and tools to leverage AI in identifying

lucrative real estate deals, evaluating investments, and managing risks effectively.

4. **Highlight Real-World Applications:** By presenting case studies and real-world examples, the guide illustrates the practical application of AI in property investment. These narratives provide tangible evidence of AI's impact, offering inspiration and lessons learned from successful AI-driven investments.

5. **Navigate Ethical and Regulatory Considerations:** Recognizing the importance of ethical and regulatory dimensions, this guide addresses potential concerns surrounding AI in real estate. It aims to foster an understanding of the ethical implications and regulatory landscape, ensuring informed and responsible use of AI technologies.

6. **Anticipate Future Trends:** Looking toward the horizon, this guide explores emerging AI trends and technologies poised to shape the future of real estate investment. It offers foresight into how investors can adapt and position themselves to capitalize on upcoming opportunities.

7. **Empower Investors to Embrace AI:** Ultimately, the purpose of this guide is to empower real estate investors to embrace AI with confidence. By providing a comprehensive overview, practical strategies, and a forward-looking perspective, it aims to inspire investors to harness AI's potential to enhance their investment journey.

In essence, this guide serves as a roadmap for investors seeking to navigate the new terrain of AI-enhanced property investment, offering insights, tools, and foresight to thrive in the dynamic landscape of real estate in 2024 and beyond.

2. Basics of AI in Real Estate

In the dawn of a new era for property markets worldwide, Artificial Intelligence (AI) stands at the forefront, redefining the boundaries of what's possible in real estate. As we embark on this journey, it's crucial to build a solid foundation of understanding. This chapter, "Basics of AI in Real Estate," is designed to introduce you to the fundamental concepts of AI, its core technologies, and how these innovations are being harnessed to transform the real estate sector.

Understanding Artificial Intelligence

At its simplest, AI involves creating computer systems that can perform tasks typically requiring human intelligence. These tasks range from recognizing patterns and learning from data to making decisions and solving complex problems. In real estate, AI translates into an ability to analyze vast amounts of data, predict trends, and offer insights that enhance decision-making.

Core Technologies Behind AI in Real Estate

Several key technologies underpin the use of AI in real estate, each contributing its unique capabilities:

1. **Machine Learning:** This technology allows computers to learn from and make predictions based on data. In real estate, machine learning algorithms can sift through historical price data, sales trends, and market conditions to identify patterns that might influence future property values or investment opportunities.

2. **Natural Language Processing (NLP):** NLP enables machines to understand and interpret human language. This is particularly useful in real estate for analyzing text-heavy data sources like property listings, legal documents, or customer inquiries to extract valuable insights.

3. **Predictive Analytics:** Leveraging historical data, predictive analytics help forecast future events. In the context of real estate, this could mean predicting which neighborhoods are likely to appreciate in value or which properties are at risk of declining prices.

4. **Computer Vision:** This technology enables computers to "see" and interpret visual information. In real estate, computer vision can analyze satellite images, property photos, or architectural plans to assess property features, conditions, or even the development potential of land.

The Role of AI in Real Estate

AI's role in real estate is multifaceted and ever-expanding. Some of the key applications include:

- **Property Valuation:** AI algorithms can quickly analyze various factors affecting property values, offering more accurate and timely appraisals.
- **Investment Analysis:** By crunching numbers on market trends, economic indicators, and property features, AI can identify high-potential investment opportunities.
- **Market Prediction:** AI's predictive capabilities enable investors to anticipate market shifts, from macroeconomic trends down to local neighborhood dynamics.

- **Operational Efficiency:** AI can streamline real estate operations, from automating routine tasks like document processing to optimizing property management and maintenance schedules.

Embracing AI in Real Estate

For investors and professionals in the real estate industry, understanding and embracing AI is no longer optional—it's essential. The insights and efficiencies AI brings to the table can significantly enhance competitive advantage, investment outcomes, and operational effectiveness.

As we delve deeper into the basics of AI in real estate, remember that this journey is about harnessing the power of technology to unlock new opportunities and navigate the complexities of the modern property market. This chapter lays the groundwork, providing you with the knowledge and perspective needed to explore the more advanced AI strategies and applications that are shaping the future of real estate investment.

What is AI and How Does it Work?

Artificial Intelligence (AI) is a branch of computer science that aims to create systems capable of performing tasks that would typically require human intelligence. These tasks include learning, decision-making, problem-solving, and understanding language. The essence of AI is not just in programming computers to follow instructions but in enabling them to learn and make decisions based on data.

How AI Works

AI works by combining large amounts of data with fast, iterative processing and intelligent algorithms, allowing the software to learn automatically from patterns or features in the data. This process is akin to the way a human learns from experience, making AI a powerful tool for handling complex tasks. Here's a closer look at how AI operates:

1. **Data Collection:** AI systems require vast amounts of data to learn. This data can come from various sources, such as text documents, images, or sensor inputs. In real estate, for example, data might include property listings, sales records, demographic information, and more.

2. **Data Processing and Analysis:** Once data is collected, AI systems use algorithms to process and analyze it. This involves identifying patterns, correlations, and trends within the data. Machine learning, a subset of AI, is particularly adept at this step, adjusting and improving its algorithms as it processes more data.

3. **Learning:** AI systems learn from data in several ways. The most common method is machine learning, where algorithms improve their performance on a specific task over time with more data. Deep learning, a subset of machine learning, uses neural networks with many layers (hence "deep") to analyze complex patterns in large data sets.

4. **Decision Making:** AI systems use the insights gained from data analysis to make decisions. In machine learning, this might involve making predictions based on new data, such as forecasting property prices or

identifying high-potential investment areas in real estate.

5. **Action:** Finally, AI systems can take action based on their analyses and decisions. In a real estate context, this could involve automating certain tasks, like generating property listings or sending alerts about new investment opportunities.

Types of AI

AI can be broadly categorized into two types:

1. **Narrow AI:** Also known as "Weak AI," this type of AI is designed to perform a narrow task (e.g., facial recognition or internet searches). Most current AI systems, including those used in real estate, fall into this category.

2. **General AI:** Also known as "Strong AI," this type of AI would have the ability to understand, learn, and apply knowledge in different contexts, much like a human being. General AI remains a goal for the future rather than a current reality.

Conclusion

AI's ability to learn from data and improve over time makes it a powerful tool across various fields, including real estate. By automating tasks, providing insights, and enhancing decision-making, AI is transforming industries and shaping the future of how we live and work. Understanding the basics of how AI functions is the first step in leveraging its potential to drive innovation and efficiency.

The Role of AI in Real Estate

Artificial Intelligence (AI) is rapidly becoming a cornerstone in the transformation of the real estate sector, offering innovative solutions to age-old challenges while unveiling new opportunities for growth and efficiency. The role of AI in real estate is multifaceted, touching upon various aspects of the industry from property discovery and valuation to market analysis and investment strategy. Here's how AI is reshaping the landscape of real estate:

Enhanced Property Discovery and Matching

AI algorithms excel at analyzing large datasets to identify patterns and preferences, making them particularly useful in matching buyers or renters with properties that meet their specific criteria. AI-driven platforms can sift through thousands of listings to recommend properties that align with the user's preferences, budget, location desires, and more, significantly streamlining the property search process.

Accurate and Dynamic Property Valuation

Traditional property valuation methods can be time-consuming and may not always account for rapid market changes. AI, through machine learning and data analytics, can assess vast amounts of real estate data, including historical sales, current listings, neighborhood trends, and economic indicators, to provide more accurate and real-time property valuations.

Predictive Market Analysis

AI's predictive analytics capabilities enable real estate professionals and investors to anticipate market trends, price movements, and potential investment hotspots. By analyzing data trends, AI can forecast future property values, rental yields, and market demand, helping investors make informed decisions and capitalize on market opportunities before they become apparent to the broader market.

Streamlined Transaction Processes

AI can automate and optimize various administrative tasks involved in real estate transactions, from document processing to due diligence checks. Smart contracts, powered by blockchain technology, can further secure transactions and automate the execution of contracts when predefined conditions are met, reducing the need for intermediaries and making transactions more efficient and transparent.

Enhanced Customer Service and Engagement

AI-powered chatbots and virtual assistants can provide 24/7 customer service, answering queries, scheduling viewings, and even offering personalized recommendations. This not only improves the customer experience but also allows real estate professionals to focus on more high-value tasks.

Innovative Property Management Solutions

For property management, AI can predict maintenance issues before they occur, optimize energy usage, and enhance security systems. By analyzing data from sensors and IoT devices, AI can help property managers and owners maintain and improve their assets more effectively.

Investment and Portfolio Optimization

AI can assist investors in identifying the best properties to add to their portfolios based on their specific goals and risk tolerance. By analyzing market data, economic indicators, and individual property performance, AI can recommend portfolio adjustments to maximize returns and minimize risks.

Ethical and Regulatory Considerations

As AI continues to permeate the real estate sector, it's essential to navigate ethical considerations, such as data privacy and bias in AI algorithms, and to stay abreast of regulatory changes that could impact the use of AI in real estate.

Conclusion

The role of AI in real estate is transformative, offering tools and insights that were unimaginable just a few decades ago. From enhancing the property search process to optimizing investment portfolios, AI is not just changing how real estate professionals operate; it's redefining the possibilities within the industry. As AI technologies continue to evolve, their impact on real estate will likely grow, making an understanding of AI an indispensable asset for industry professionals.

3. Starting with AI: What You Need to Know

Embarking on the journey of integrating Artificial Intelligence (AI) into real estate ventures can be both exhilarating and daunting. As the digital and physical realms of property investment converge, understanding the fundamentals of AI becomes paramount. This chapter aims to equip you with the essential knowledge needed to begin leveraging AI in real estate, providing a clear roadmap for harnessing its potential to transform your investment strategies and operations.

Understanding the Basics

Before diving into the intricacies of AI applications, it's crucial to grasp the basic concepts that underpin AI technology. AI involves creating systems capable of performing tasks that typically require human intelligence, such as learning from data, recognizing patterns, making decisions, and solving problems. Key components include Machine Learning (ML), Natural Language Processing (NLP), and data analytics, each playing a vital role in interpreting and utilizing vast amounts of real estate data.

Identifying Your AI Goals

The first step in starting with AI is to identify specific goals you aim to achieve by incorporating AI into your real estate operations. Whether it's improving property valuation accuracy, streamlining transaction processes, enhancing customer engagement, or optimizing investment strategies, having clear objectives will guide your AI integration efforts and help measure success.

Gathering and Preparing Data

AI thrives on data. The quality and quantity of data you have access to will significantly impact the effectiveness of AI applications. Start by auditing your current data sources, including property listings, transaction records, customer interactions, market reports, and more. Ensuring data is clean, organized, and accessible is crucial for training AI models and deriving meaningful insights.

Choosing the Right AI Tools and Platforms

The market is teeming with AI tools and platforms, each offering a range of functionalities tailored to different aspects of real estate. Evaluate these options based on your specific goals, the ease of integration into your existing systems, scalability, and cost. Consider starting with user-friendly platforms that offer robust support and resources to help you navigate the initial learning curve.

Building or Partnering for AI Solutions

Depending on your resources and technical expertise, you may choose to develop custom AI solutions in-house or partner with AI service providers. Building in-house offers greater control and customization but requires significant investment in talent and technology. Partnering, on the other hand, allows you to leverage existing AI solutions and expertise, providing a more cost-effective and time-efficient path to integration.

Understanding Ethical and Legal Implications

As you embark on integrating AI into your real estate business, it's crucial to consider the ethical and legal implications. Ensure that your use of AI respects privacy laws, data protection regulations, and ethical standards. Being transparent about how AI is used in your operations can build trust with clients and stakeholders.

Fostering an AI-Ready Culture

Integrating AI into your real estate operations goes beyond technology; it requires cultivating an AI-ready culture within your organization. Educate your team about the benefits and implications of AI, encourage open communication about AI initiatives, and foster a culture of continuous learning and innovation.

Continuous Learning and Adaptation

The field of AI is continuously evolving, with new developments and applications emerging regularly. Staying informed about the latest trends, technologies, and best practices in AI and real estate will enable you to adapt your strategies and maintain a competitive edge.

Conclusion

Starting with AI in real estate is a journey of transformation, offering the promise of enhanced efficiency, accuracy, and insights. By understanding the basics of AI, setting clear objectives, preparing your data, choosing the right tools, and fostering an AI-ready culture, you can navigate the complexities of AI integration and unlock new opportunities in the real estate sector. As you embark on this journey, remember that the ultimate goal is not just to adopt AI for its own sake but to leverage its potential to drive meaningful improvements in your real estate endeavors.

Key AI Concepts for Real Estate Investors

As real estate investors navigate the evolving landscape of property investment, understanding key AI concepts is essential. These concepts not only illuminate the capabilities of AI but also how it can be leveraged to enhance investment strategies, risk assessment, and market analysis. Here are the fundamental AI concepts that every real estate investor should be familiar with:

Machine Learning (ML)

Machine Learning, a subset of AI, involves algorithms that enable computers to learn from and make predictions or decisions based on data. In real estate, ML can analyze historical transaction data, price trends, and market dynamics to identify patterns that inform investment decisions. For investors, understanding the basics of ML models, such as regression analysis for price predictions or classification algorithms for identifying investment grades of properties, is invaluable.

Natural Language Processing (NLP)

NLP enables machines to understand and interpret human language. For real estate investors, NLP can be a game-changer in analyzing sentiment in news articles, social media, and market reports, providing insights into market trends and consumer sentiment. Familiarity with NLP applications can help investors gauge public perception and potential market movements.

Predictive Analytics

Predictive analytics uses historical data, statistical algorithms, and ML techniques to forecast future events. Real estate investors can use predictive analytics to anticipate market trends, property value fluctuations, and investment risk levels. Understanding how predictive models are constructed and interpreted can significantly enhance an investor's ability to make data-driven decisions.

Big Data

Big Data refers to extremely large data sets that may be analyzed computationally to reveal patterns, trends, and associations. In real estate, big data encompasses everything from property listings and transaction histories to demographic and economic indicators. Investors should grasp how big data can be harnessed to extract meaningful insights about investment opportunities and market conditions.

Data Mining

Data mining is the process of discovering patterns and knowledge from large amounts of data. The data source could be databases, data warehouses, the internet, or any other information repository. Real estate investors can use data mining techniques to identify potential investment properties, evaluate market conditions, and understand consumer behavior.

Artificial Neural Networks (ANN)

Inspired by the biological neural networks that constitute animal brains, ANNs are a subset of ML and are at the heart of deep learning algorithms. They are particularly useful in real estate for complex pattern recognition, such as image analysis for property assessment or automated valuation models. Investors with an understanding of ANN capabilities can leverage them for more nuanced property evaluations and market analyses.

Geographic Information Systems (GIS)

GIS is a framework for gathering, managing, and analyzing geographic data. For real estate investors, GIS can be instrumental in visualizing spatial data, such as property locations, neighborhood characteristics, and geographical factors affecting property values. Knowledge of GIS applications can aid investors in identifying geographically advantageous investment opportunities.

Blockchain and Smart Contracts

Blockchain technology offers a secure, transparent way to record transactions, and smart contracts automate contractual obligations. In real estate, this can streamline transactions, reduce fraud, and increase transparency. Investors should be aware of how blockchain and smart contracts can impact investment processes and property management.

Ethics and Bias in AI

Understanding the ethical considerations and potential biases in AI algorithms is crucial for real estate investors. Ensuring that AI tools are used responsibly and that investment decisions are free from algorithmic bias is essential for maintaining fairness and integrity in the market.

Conclusion

For real estate investors, mastering these key AI concepts is not just about keeping pace with technological advancements; it's about leveraging these technologies to uncover deeper market insights, improve investment strategies, and navigate the complexities of the real estate market with greater confidence and foresight. As AI continues to shape the future of real estate, investors equipped with this knowledge will be well-positioned to capitalize on the opportunities that AI-driven insights and tools present.

Understanding Data: The Foundation of AI

In the realm of Artificial Intelligence (AI), data acts as the lifeblood that fuels innovation, insights, and advancements. For real estate investors venturing into AI-enhanced strategies, comprehending the pivotal role of data is essential. This foundation not only powers AI systems but also shapes their accuracy, reliability, and effectiveness. Here, we delve into the core aspects of data in AI, highlighting its significance and how it can be leveraged in the context of real estate investment.

The Centrality of Data in AI

AI algorithms, from basic machine learning models to advanced neural networks, rely heavily on data for training, learning, and evolving. The quality, diversity, and volume of data directly influence an AI system's ability to make accurate predictions, identify patterns, and provide actionable insights. In real estate, this could range from predicting property values to identifying emerging market trends.

Types of Data in Real Estate

Real estate data can be broadly categorized into structured and unstructured forms:

- **Structured Data:** This includes quantitative or categorical data that is organized in a fixed format, making it easily searchable and understandable by AI algorithms. Examples in real estate include property prices, square footage, number of bedrooms, and transaction dates.
- **Unstructured Data:** This encompasses more complex information that doesn't fit into predefined data models, such as textual descriptions, images, videos, and social media posts. For real estate, unstructured data could include property listing descriptions, architectural plans, or customer reviews.

Sources of Real Estate Data

Data for real estate AI applications can be sourced from a multitude of channels:

- **Property Listings and Databases:** Online listings, MLS databases, and property records provide a wealth of structured data.
- **Government and Public Records:** Tax assessments, zoning information, and public infrastructure data offer insights into property valuations and urban development.
- **Social Media and Online Platforms:** User-generated content on platforms like Twitter, Facebook, and real estate forums can provide valuable unstructured data on market sentiment and trends.
- **Geospatial Data:** Satellite images and geographic information systems (GIS) data offer spatial insights into property locations, neighborhood amenities, and environmental factors.

Data Quality and Preparation

The adage "garbage in, garbage out" holds particularly true in AI. High-quality data is paramount for training effective AI models. Real estate investors must ensure their data is:

- **Accurate:** Free from errors and discrepancies.
- **Complete:** Lacking no critical values or information.
- **Consistent:** Uniform in format and representation across the dataset.
- **Relevant:** Directly applicable and useful for the task at hand.

Preparing data for AI involves cleaning (removing inaccuracies or duplicates), normalization (scaling data to a standard range), and feature engineering (creating new variables from existing data to improve model performance).

Ethical Considerations and Data Privacy

As investors harness data for AI in real estate, ethical considerations around data privacy, consent, and security become paramount. Adhering to regulations like GDPR in Europe or CCPA in California is not just about compliance but about building trust and ensuring the responsible use of data.

Leveraging Data for AI in Real Estate

For real estate investors, effectively leveraging data involves:

- **Integrating Diverse Data Sources:** Combining various data types and sources can provide a more holistic view of the market and investment opportunities.
- **Continuous Data Collection:** Real estate markets are dynamic; continuous data collection ensures AI models remain relevant and accurate.
- **Collaborating with Data Scientists:** Working with experts who can manipulate and analyze complex datasets can unlock deeper insights and more sophisticated AI applications.

Conclusion

Understanding and effectively managing data is foundational for real estate investors looking to leverage AI. By prioritizing data quality, embracing diverse data sources, and adhering to ethical standards, investors can empower AI systems to deliver transformative insights and drive smarter, more informed investment decisions in the ever-evolving landscape of real estate.

4. AI Tools for Finding Real Estate Deals

In the competitive realm of real estate investing, Artificial Intelligence (AI) tools have emerged as game-changers, offering investors unprecedented advantages in identifying lucrative deals. This chapter delves into the variety of AI tools specifically designed to uncover real estate opportunities, highlighting how they work, their applications, and the benefits they bring to the table for savvy investors.

AI-Driven Property Search Platforms

AI-powered search platforms revolutionize how investors find properties by leveraging advanced algorithms to match user preferences with available listings. These platforms analyze vast amounts of data, including price trends, location preferences, and desired property features, to recommend properties that align closely with investors' criteria.

Key Features:

- Personalized property recommendations
- Predictive search capabilities based on user behavior
- Integration with market data for real-time insights

Predictive Analytics Tools

Predictive analytics tools utilize historical data and machine learning algorithms to forecast future market trends, property valuations, and investment risks. These tools can predict which neighborhoods are likely to appreciate in value or which types of properties are poised for high rental yields.

Key Features:

- Market trend analysis and forecasting
- Property value predictions based on historical data
- Risk assessment models for different investment scenarios

Automated Valuation Models (AVMs)

AVMs use AI to assess property values quickly and accurately. By analyzing data points such as recent sales, property characteristics, and market conditions, AVMs provide investors with instant property valuations, helping them make informed decisions swiftly.

Key Features:

- Instant property valuations
- Comparative market analysis
- Integration with property databases for comprehensive evaluations

Chatbots and Virtual Assistants

AI-powered chatbots and virtual assistants enhance customer engagement by providing instant responses to investor queries, scheduling property viewings, and even offering investment advice. These tools are available 24/7, ensuring that investors have access to information and support whenever needed.

Key Features:

- Instant communication and query resolution
- Scheduling and reminders for property viewings
- Personalized investment advice and insights

Investment Portfolio Optimization Tools

AI tools designed for investment portfolio optimization analyze market data, investor preferences, and financial goals to recommend the most suitable properties for portfolio inclusion. These tools can balance risk and return, ensuring that investors' portfolios are diversified and aligned with their investment strategies.

Key Features:

- Portfolio diversification analysis
- Risk-return optimization
- Dynamic portfolio recommendations based on market conditions

Real Estate Marketplaces with AI Capabilities

Online real estate marketplaces are increasingly integrating AI features to enhance user experiences. These platforms offer advanced filtering, sorting, and recommendation features, making it easier for investors to navigate listings and identify potential deals.

Key Features:

- Enhanced search and filtering options

- AI-driven property recommendations
- Market insights and analytics

Geospatial Analysis Tools

Leveraging Geographic Information Systems (GIS) and AI, geospatial analysis tools provide investors with a spatial perspective on real estate investments. These tools can identify location-based trends, such as demographic shifts or infrastructure developments, that might impact property values.

Key Features:

- Mapping and visualization of real estate data
- Analysis of location-based trends and factors
- Integration with demographic and economic data

Social Media and Sentiment Analysis Tools

By analyzing social media data and online sentiment, these tools offer insights into public perception and emerging trends in real estate. Investors can gauge market sentiment towards specific neighborhoods, developments, or property types, informing their investment decisions.

Key Features:

- Analysis of social media trends and sentiment
- Identification of emerging real estate trends
- Insights into public perception of property markets

Conclusion

AI tools are transforming the landscape of real estate investing, providing investors with powerful capabilities to find and evaluate deals. From predictive analytics and automated valuations to geospatial analysis and social media insights, these tools offer a competitive edge in the fast-paced world of real estate. By leveraging AI, investors can make data-driven decisions, optimize their portfolios, and stay ahead in the game, ensuring they capitalize on the best investment opportunities the market has to offer.

Overview of AI Tools and Platforms

The integration of Artificial Intelligence (AI) in various sectors has led to the development of numerous tools and platforms, each designed to enhance efficiency, accuracy, and decision-making processes. In the realm of real estate, AI tools and platforms are particularly transformative, offering innovative solutions for market analysis, property valuation, investment strategy, and customer engagement. This section provides an overview of the diverse landscape of AI tools and platforms, highlighting their functionalities and how they are revolutionizing industries, including real estate.

Data Analytics and Predictive Modeling Platforms

These platforms harness the power of AI to analyze large datasets, identifying patterns, trends, and correlations. In real estate, they can predict market movements, property value changes, and investment risks.

- **Examples:** IBM Watson, Google Cloud AI, and Salesforce Einstein offer robust analytics capabilities, empowering users to derive actionable insights from complex data.

Machine Learning Frameworks

Machine learning frameworks are essential for developing AI models that can learn from data, improve over time, and make predictions or decisions.

- **Examples:** TensorFlow and PyTorch are popular frameworks that facilitate the creation and training of machine learning models, applicable in various fields including finance, healthcare, and real estate for tasks like price prediction and trend analysis.

Natural Language Processing (NLP) Tools

NLP tools enable machines to understand, interpret, and generate human language, making them invaluable for analyzing textual data, automating customer service, and extracting insights from unstructured data.

- **Examples:** OpenAI's GPT (Generative Pretrained Transformer) series and Google's BERT are leading NLP models that can be applied in chatbots, sentiment analysis, and content generation.

Computer Vision Platforms

Computer vision platforms allow machines to interpret and analyze visual data from the world. In real estate, this could involve analyzing property images for features, condition assessment, or even identifying locations from satellite imagery.

- **Examples:** Amazon Rekognition and Microsoft Azure Computer Vision provide powerful image and video analysis capabilities for various applications, including security, marketing, and property assessment.

Geospatial Analysis Tools

These tools integrate AI with geographic information systems (GIS) to analyze and visualize spatial data, offering insights into location trends, demographic changes, and environmental impacts on properties.

- **Examples:** ESRI's ArcGIS uses AI for advanced spatial analysis, helping real estate professionals in site selection, market analysis, and urban planning.

AI-Enabled Real Estate Platforms

Several platforms specifically cater to the real estate industry, incorporating AI to streamline property search, valuation, and transaction processes, among other functionalities.

- **Examples:** Zillow and Redfin utilize AI for property recommendations, price estimations, and market trend analysis, enhancing the property buying and selling experience for users.

Investment and Portfolio Management Tools

AI-driven tools for investment and portfolio management analyze market data, investor profiles, and financial goals to provide personalized investment recommendations and risk assessments.

- **Examples:** Roofstock and Fundrise leverage AI to offer tailored real estate investment opportunities, optimizing portfolios for maximum returns and minimal risks.

Blockchain and Smart Contracts

While not AI tools per se, blockchain technology and smart contracts are often integrated with AI to enhance security, transparency, and efficiency in transactions and contracts.

- **Examples:** Propy and RealT utilize blockchain to secure real estate transactions, with AI potentially playing a role in automating and optimizing contract terms based on data analysis.

Conclusion

The landscape of AI tools and platforms is vast and varied, with each offering unique capabilities that can be harnessed across different industries, including real estate. Whether it's through predictive analytics, machine learning, NLP, or computer vision, AI is enabling more informed decision-making, operational efficiency, and enhanced customer experiences. As these technologies continue to evolve, their impact is set to deepen, further transforming how businesses and industries operate.

How AI Identifies Potential Deals

Artificial Intelligence (AI) is revolutionizing the way real estate professionals and investors identify potential deals. By harnessing vast amounts of data and employing sophisticated algorithms, AI can uncover investment opportunities that might otherwise remain hidden. This process involves several key mechanisms and technologies that work together to analyze market trends, property data, and economic indicators, ultimately providing actionable insights. Here's how AI identifies potential real estate deals:

Data Aggregation and Analysis

AI systems start by aggregating massive datasets from various sources, including MLS listings, public property records, economic reports, social media, and more. This data encompasses both structured information (like property prices, square footage, and location) and unstructured data (such as property descriptions and images). Machine Learning (ML) algorithms then analyze this data to identify patterns, correlations, and anomalies that could indicate potential investment opportunities.

Predictive Analytics

One of the most powerful aspects of AI in real estate is predictive analytics. AI uses historical data and current market trends to forecast future property values, rental yields, and market demand. By applying predictive models, AI can highlight properties and areas likely to experience appreciation, offering investors a chance to buy in before prices surge.

Machine Learning Models

Machine learning models, particularly regression analysis and decision trees, are adept at analyzing complex, multifaceted data sets. In real estate, these models can evaluate numerous variables simultaneously, such as location desirability, property condition, market saturation, and more, to assess the potential profitability of a property or project.

Natural Language Processing (NLP)

NLP allows AI to understand and interpret human language, making it invaluable for analyzing textual data in property listings, news articles, and online discussions. By parsing this text, AI can extract insights about market sentiment, emerging trends, and consumer preferences, which can signal potential investment opportunities.

Geospatial Analysis

Integrating AI with Geographic Information Systems (GIS) enables the analysis of geographical and spatial data. AI can identify emerging markets, up-and-coming neighborhoods, and areas with high development potential by examining factors like infrastructure developments, demographic shifts, and proximity to amenities.

Image and Pattern Recognition

AI-powered computer vision technologies can analyze property images and satellite photos to assess a property's condition, features, and surrounding area. This analysis can reveal undervalued properties that, with minor improvements, could significantly increase in value.

Market Sentiment Analysis

By monitoring and analyzing social media chatter, news sentiment, and online forums, AI can gauge public sentiment towards specific real estate markets, developments, or property types. Positive sentiment can indicate rising interest and potential for value appreciation, highlighting promising investment opportunities.

Real-Time Data Processing

AI's ability to process and analyze data in real time ensures that investors receive timely, relevant insights. This capability allows for quick identification of potential deals as soon as they emerge, providing a competitive edge in fast-moving markets.

Integration with Financial Models

AI can integrate real estate data with financial models to assess the viability of potential investments. By considering factors like cash flow, financing options, and economic conditions, AI can help investors identify deals that align with their investment strategies and financial goals.

Conclusion

AI identifies potential real estate deals by leveraging a combination of data analysis, predictive analytics, machine learning, and other advanced technologies. This multifaceted approach enables investors to uncover hidden opportunities, make data-driven decisions, and stay ahead in the competitive real estate market. As AI technologies continue to advance, their capacity to identify and evaluate investment opportunities will only become more sophisticated, further transforming the landscape of real estate investing.

5. Using AI to Analyze Market Trends

The ability to accurately analyze and predict market trends is crucial for success in real estate investment. Artificial Intelligence (AI) has become an indispensable tool in this endeavor, offering insights that were previously unattainable due to the sheer volume and complexity of data involved. This chapter delves into how AI is used to dissect and understand market trends, providing investors with a strategic edge in making informed decisions.

Harnessing Big Data for Market Insights

AI's capability to process and analyze big data sets it apart in market trend analysis. By aggregating data from multiple sources, including property listings, transaction records, economic indicators, and even social media, AI provides a comprehensive view of the market. This big-picture perspective is essential for identifying overarching trends and subtle shifts that could influence investment strategies.

Predictive Analytics and Forecasting

At the core of AI's value in market analysis is predictive analytics. By applying machine learning algorithms to historical and current data, AI can forecast future market movements, such as shifts in property prices, rental demand, and inventory levels. These predictions allow investors to anticipate market changes and position their portfolios accordingly.

Machine Learning Models for Trend Identification

Machine learning models, including time-series analysis and regression models, are particularly adept at identifying patterns and trends within complex data sets. In real estate, these models analyze variables such as historical price changes, supply-demand dynamics, and demographic shifts to pinpoint emerging market trends.

Natural Language Processing for Sentiment Analysis

Natural Language Processing (NLP) enables AI to interpret human language, making it invaluable for sentiment analysis. By examining news articles, blog posts, and social media content, AI can gauge public sentiment towards various market segments, identifying areas of growing interest or concern that could impact market trends.

Real-Time Market Monitoring

One of AI's most significant advantages is its ability to monitor markets in real time. This capability ensures that investors have access to the latest data, enabling them to react swiftly to new developments. Real-time monitoring is particularly useful in volatile markets, where conditions can change rapidly.

Comparative Market Analysis (CMA)

AI enhances Comparative Market Analysis by automating the process of comparing similar properties in a given area. This analysis provides insights into fair market prices, rental rates, and property features that are in demand, helping investors make pricing decisions and identify attractive investment properties.

Geospatial Analysis for Location Insights

Integrating AI with Geographic Information Systems (GIS) offers spatial analysis capabilities, enabling investors to evaluate how location impacts market trends. Factors such as proximity to amenities, infrastructure developments, and neighborhood demographics are analyzed to understand their influence on property values and market dynamics.

Integration with Economic Models

AI tools often integrate real estate data with broader economic models to provide context for market trends. By considering factors like interest rates, employment data, and GDP growth, AI can help investors understand how macroeconomic conditions influence real estate markets.

Customizable Dashboards and Reporting

AI platforms offer customizable dashboards and reporting tools, allowing investors to focus on metrics and trends most relevant to their investment strategies. These tools provide a personalized view of the market, highlighting opportunities and risks tailored to individual investment goals.

Conclusion

Using AI to analyze market trends equips real estate investors with deep, actionable insights that go beyond traditional analysis methods. By leveraging big data, predictive analytics, and real-time monitoring, AI provides a nuanced understanding of market dynamics, empowering investors to make data-driven decisions. As AI technologies continue to evolve, their role in market trend analysis will only grow, further enhancing their value to the real estate investment community.

Predictive Analytics for Real Estate

Predictive analytics in real estate harnesses the power of data, statistical algorithms, and machine learning techniques to forecast future trends, property values, and market dynamics. This forward-looking approach provides real estate professionals and investors with invaluable insights, enabling them to anticipate changes in the market, identify investment opportunities, and make informed decisions. This chapter explores the key aspects of predictive analytics in real estate, its applications, and the transformative impact it has on the industry.

Fundamentals of Predictive Analytics

Predictive analytics involves analyzing historical and current data to make predictions about future events. In real estate, this can range from forecasting property prices and rental yields to anticipating market demand and identifying emerging trends. The process involves several steps:

1. **Data Collection:** Gathering comprehensive data from various sources, including property listings, sales transactions, economic indicators, and demographic trends.

2. **Data Cleaning and Preparation:** Ensuring the data is accurate, consistent, and formatted correctly for analysis.

3. **Model Selection:** Choosing appropriate statistical or machine learning models that best fit the data and the prediction objectives.

4. **Model Training:** Using historical data to train the model, allowing it to learn and identify patterns and relationships within the data.

5. **Validation and Testing:** Assessing the model's accuracy and reliability using a separate dataset not used during the training phase.

6. **Prediction:** Applying the trained model to current data to make predictions about future real estate trends and values.

Applications in Real Estate

Predictive analytics finds numerous applications in real estate, each offering unique insights and advantages:

- **Property Valuation:** Predictive models can estimate future property values based on factors like historical price trends, location characteristics, and market conditions, helping investors assess potential returns on investments.

- **Market Trend Analysis:** By analyzing past and present market data, predictive analytics can identify trends, such as which neighborhoods are gaining popularity or what property types are in demand, guiding investors toward promising opportunities.

- **Risk Assessment:** Predictive models can evaluate the risks associated with different investment properties or strategies by considering factors like market volatility, economic shifts, and property-specific issues.

- **Demand Forecasting:** Predictive analytics can forecast future demand for various types of properties in different locations, enabling developers and investors to make strategic decisions about where and what to build.
- **Investment Optimization:** By predicting future market conditions and property performances, predictive analytics can help investors optimize their portfolios for maximum returns and minimized risks.

Advantages of Predictive Analytics

The use of predictive analytics in real estate offers several key advantages:

- **Informed Decision-Making:** Provides data-driven insights that enhance the decision-making process, reducing reliance on intuition and speculation.
- **Competitive Edge:** Offers a deeper understanding of market dynamics and future trends, giving investors a competitive advantage in identifying and capitalizing on opportunities.
- **Risk Mitigation:** Helps identify and assess potential risks, allowing investors to take proactive measures to mitigate them.
- **Efficiency and Productivity:** Automates the analysis of vast amounts of data, saving time and resources while increasing productivity.
- **Personalization and Targeting:** Enables real estate professionals to tailor their services and offerings to meet the specific needs and preferences of their clients.

Challenges and Considerations

While predictive analytics offers significant benefits, it also comes with challenges:

- **Data Quality and Availability:** The accuracy of predictions is heavily dependent on the quality and comprehensiveness of the data used.
- **Model Complexity:** Developing and fine-tuning predictive models can be complex and requires expertise in data science and machine learning.
- **Changing Market Conditions:** Real estate markets can be influenced by numerous unpredictable factors, making it challenging to account for all variables in predictive models.
- **Ethical and Privacy Concerns:** The use of personal and sensitive data in predictive analytics raises ethical and privacy concerns that must be addressed responsibly.

Conclusion

Predictive analytics is reshaping the landscape of real estate, offering unprecedented insights and capabilities to professionals and investors. By leveraging historical and current data to forecast future trends and values, predictive analytics enables more strategic, informed, and effective real estate decisions. As technology and data availability continue to advance, the role of predictive analytics in real estate is set to become even more pivotal, driving innovation and success in the industry.

Case Studies: AI Predicting Market Shifts

The application of Artificial Intelligence (AI) in predicting real estate market shifts has provided tangible benefits and insights across various regions and market segments. These case studies illustrate the power of AI in forecasting market trends, enabling investors and professionals to navigate the complexities of the real estate market with greater precision and foresight.

Case Study 1: Urban Revitalization and Emerging Neighborhoods

Background: In a major metropolitan area, real estate professionals sought to identify emerging neighborhoods poised for growth and revitalization.

AI Application: Utilizing machine learning algorithms, AI analyzed vast amounts of data, including property transactions, demographic changes, infrastructure developments, and social media sentiment.

Outcome: The AI model successfully identified several neighborhoods experiencing an uptick in investment, cultural activities, and population growth. Real estate investors who capitalized on this information acquired properties at lower prices before the market peaked, resulting in substantial returns as the neighborhoods became more desirable.

Case Study 2: Predicting the Impact of Economic Changes

Background: With an impending change in economic policy expected to impact interest rates and housing affordability, investors needed to understand the potential effects on the real estate market.

AI Application: An AI system employed predictive analytics to model various scenarios based on historical data, economic indicators, and proposed policy changes.

Outcome: The model predicted a short-term slowdown in high-end property sales and an increased demand for rental properties. Investors adjusted their strategies accordingly, focusing more on rental investments, which paid off as the predictions came to fruition.

Case Study 3: Commercial Real Estate and Post-Pandemic Recovery

Background: In the wake of the COVID-19 pandemic, commercial real estate investors faced significant uncertainty regarding office spaces and retail locations.

AI Application: AI tools analyzed trends in remote work, e-commerce growth, and foot traffic data in commercial areas to forecast the recovery and transformation of commercial real estate.

Outcome: The AI models predicted a shift towards mixed-use developments and an increased demand for flexible office spaces. Investors who adapted their portfolios to include such properties benefited from early investments in these emerging trends.

Case Study 4: Global Investment Opportunities and Market Diversification

Background: A global real estate investment firm sought to diversify its portfolio by identifying undervalued markets with growth potential worldwide.

AI Application: Leveraging geospatial analysis and global market data, AI algorithms evaluated political stability, economic growth, urban development, and real estate market maturity to pinpoint promising investment locations.

Outcome: The firm successfully identified and invested in several markets that were on the cusp of real estate booms, thanks to infrastructure projects and economic reforms, diversifying its portfolio and reducing risk.

Case Study 5: Climate Change and Long-Term Property Valuation

Background: With growing concerns about climate change, investors needed to assess the long-term impact on property values in coastal areas prone to rising sea levels and extreme weather events.

AI Application: AI models incorporated climate data, environmental risk assessments, and property valuations to predict how changing environmental conditions could affect property values over time.

Outcome: The predictions enabled investors to make informed decisions about divesting from high-risk areas and investing in properties with lower environmental risks, safeguarding their portfolios against future climate-related challenges.

Conclusion

These case studies demonstrate the diverse applications and significant impact of AI in predicting real estate market shifts. By harnessing the power of AI, investors and professionals can gain a competitive edge, making data-driven decisions that align with emerging trends and market dynamics. As AI technology continues to evolve, its role in forecasting and navigating market shifts will become increasingly vital in the strategic planning and success of real estate investments.

6. AI in Property Valuation

The advent of Artificial Intelligence (AI) in property valuation has marked a transformative shift in the real estate industry. This chapter delves into how AI is revolutionizing property appraisal processes, offering accuracy, efficiency, and depth of insight that traditional methods can seldom match. We explore the mechanics, applications, and implications of AI-driven valuations, underscoring how this technology is reshaping the landscape of real estate investment and management.

The Mechanism Behind AI-Driven Valuations

AI in property valuation primarily leverages machine learning algorithms to analyze vast datasets, including historical transaction records, property features, market trends, and even socio-economic indicators. This data-driven approach allows AI models to identify patterns and correlations that human appraisers might overlook, providing a more nuanced understanding of a property's value.

1. **Automated Valuation Models (AVM):** AVMs are at the forefront of AI in property valuation. These models use statistical techniques to assess the value of a property by comparing it with similar properties (comparables) and considering various influencing factors.

2. **Deep Learning for Feature Analysis:** Deep learning, a subset of machine learning, is used to analyze property images and extract features such as property condition,

architectural style, and landscaping, which can significantly impact valuation.
3. **Natural Language Processing (NLP):** NLP techniques are employed to analyze property descriptions, listing details, and even neighborhood reviews to glean insights that contribute to the valuation process.

Applications of AI in Property Valuation

AI-driven property valuation finds application across various facets of real estate, from residential to commercial sectors:

- **Real Estate Transactions:** AI enhances the speed and accuracy of property appraisals, facilitating quicker transactions and reducing bottlenecks in the buying and selling process.
- **Investment Analysis:** Investors utilize AI valuations to assess potential returns, compare investment opportunities, and make data-driven decisions.
- **Portfolio Management:** For portfolio managers, AI-driven valuations offer a real-time view of asset values, enabling dynamic portfolio optimization and risk assessment.
- **Insurance and Taxation:** Insurers and tax assessors leverage AI valuations for accurate property assessments, ensuring fair premiums and tax evaluations.

Advantages of AI in Property Valuation

The integration of AI into property valuation processes brings several distinct advantages:

- **Speed and Efficiency:** AI can process and analyze data at a scale and speed unattainable by human appraisers, significantly reducing the time required for valuations.
- **Accuracy and Consistency:** By minimizing human error and bias, AI ensures more consistent and objective property valuations.
- **Comprehensive Analysis:** AI models can consider a broader range of factors, including market trends, economic indicators, and even environmental risks, providing a holistic view of a property's value.
- **Scalability:** AI-driven valuation tools can easily scale to handle large volumes of appraisals, making them ideal for large real estate firms and financial institutions.

Challenges and Ethical Considerations

Despite its advantages, AI in property valuation is not without challenges:

- **Data Quality and Availability:** The accuracy of AI valuations heavily depends on the quality and comprehensiveness of the underlying data.
- **Transparency and Explainability:** AI valuation models, especially those based on deep learning, can be complex and opaque, making it difficult to understand how valuations are derived.
- **Regulatory Compliance:** Ensuring that AI-driven valuation tools comply with local and international appraisal standards and regulations is crucial.
- **Bias and Fairness:** AI models can inadvertently perpetuate biases present in historical data, necessitating careful design and regular auditing to ensure fairness.

The Future of AI in Property Valuation

The trajectory of AI in property valuation points towards even greater integration and sophistication. Future developments may include enhanced predictive analytics for forecasting property value trends, integration with blockchain for transparent and secure valuation records, and the adoption of AI-driven valuation tools as industry standards.

Conclusion

AI has undeniably transformed the practice of property valuation, offering tools that blend speed, accuracy, and depth of analysis. As the technology continues to evolve, its potential to further refine and revolutionize real estate appraisals remains vast. For real estate professionals, investors, and financial institutions, understanding and leveraging AI in property valuation is becoming increasingly essential in navigating the complexities of the modern real estate market.

Automated Valuation Models (AVMs)

Automated Valuation Models (AVMs) represent a significant technological advancement in the realm of real estate, employing sophisticated algorithms to estimate property values swiftly and objectively. These models harness vast amounts of data, including historical sales, property characteristics, market trends, and geographical information, to generate accurate property valuations. This chapter delves into the intricacies of AVMs, exploring their methodology, applications, benefits, and limitations within the real estate industry.

Understanding AVMs

AVMs are computer-based systems that analyze various data points to determine a property's market value without the need for a physical inspection. They rely on mathematical modeling to assess real estate properties, considering factors such as:

- **Property Characteristics:** Size, age, condition, and unique features of the property.
- **Comparative Market Analysis:** Prices of similar properties in the vicinity.
- **Market Trends:** Current market conditions and historical price trends.
- **Location Factors:** Proximity to amenities, schools, transportation, and other locational attributes.

Methodology of AVMs

The core of AVM functionality lies in its algorithmic approach, which typically involves:

1. **Data Collection:** Gathering extensive data from public records, real estate databases, and MLS listings.
2. **Data Analysis:** Employing statistical and machine learning techniques to identify patterns and relationships within the data.
3. **Modeling:** Developing predictive models that can estimate property values based on identified patterns and correlations.
4. **Validation:** Continuously testing and refining the models against actual market transactions to ensure accuracy and reliability.

Applications of AVMs

AVMs find utility across various sectors of the real estate industry:

- **Lending Institutions:** Banks and mortgage lenders use AVMs for quick property valuations during the loan origination and refinancing processes.
- **Real Estate Professionals:** Agents and brokers leverage AVMs to price listings accurately and counsel clients on buying or selling prices.
- **Investors:** Real estate investors utilize AVMs to assess potential investments, analyze market conditions, and make informed decisions.
- **Appraisal Firms:** Appraisers incorporate AVMs to enhance the efficiency and accuracy of traditional appraisal methods.

Benefits of Using AVMs

AVMs offer several advantages that make them a valuable tool in real estate valuation:

- **Speed:** AVMs can deliver property valuations in a matter of seconds, significantly faster than traditional appraisal methods.
- **Cost-Effectiveness:** They reduce the cost associated with property valuations by minimizing the need for physical inspections and manual analysis.
- **Objectivity:** AVMs provide unbiased estimates based on data and algorithms, eliminating human error and subjectivity.

- **Scalability:** Capable of processing a large volume of valuations simultaneously, AVMs are ideal for portfolio analysis and mass appraisal tasks.

Limitations and Challenges

Despite their advantages, AVMs also face certain limitations:

- **Data Dependency:** The accuracy of AVMs is heavily reliant on the quality, completeness, and currency of the underlying data.
- **Market Variability:** AVMs may struggle to accurately value properties in less active or more volatile markets due to limited or fluctuating data.
- **Unique Properties:** Properties with unique features or those that lack comparable market data can pose challenges for AVM accuracy.
- **Regulatory Compliance:** Ensuring that AVMs meet industry standards and regulatory requirements is essential for their acceptance and use.

The Future of AVMs

As technology advances, AVMs are expected to become more sophisticated, incorporating real-time data, advanced machine learning algorithms, and even AI-driven insights to improve accuracy and applicability. The integration of AVMs with other technologies like blockchain for transparency and IoT for real-time property data collection could further enhance their capabilities and reliability.

Conclusion

Automated Valuation Models have transformed the landscape of property valuation, offering a fast, cost-effective, and objective alternative to traditional appraisal methods. While they present certain challenges, ongoing advancements in data analytics and AI promise to mitigate these limitations, making AVMs an increasingly indispensable tool in the real estate industry.

Accuracy and Reliability of AI Valuations

The adoption of Artificial Intelligence (AI) in property valuations has introduced a paradigm shift in the real estate industry, offering rapid and cost-effective estimations. However, the accuracy and reliability of these AI-driven valuations are critical for their credibility and widespread acceptance. This chapter examines the factors influencing the precision of AI valuations, the challenges faced, and strategies to enhance their dependability.

Factors Influencing AI Valuation Accuracy

1. **Data Quality and Volume:** The foundation of AI's accuracy lies in the data it analyzes. High-quality, comprehensive, and current data ensures more precise valuations. Conversely, incomplete, outdated, or inaccurate data can lead to erroneous estimates.
2. **Algorithm Complexity and Sophistication:** The algorithms underlying AI valuations, from simple linear regression models to complex neural networks, significantly impact their accuracy. Advanced models

that can analyze complex patterns and relationships tend to provide more reliable estimates.

3. **Market Dynamics and Volatility:** AI systems' ability to adapt to rapidly changing market conditions affects their precision. In stable markets, AI valuations tend to be more accurate, whereas in volatile markets, their reliability can be compromised.

4. **Property Uniqueness and Comparability:** AI valuations are most accurate for properties with ample comparable data. Unique properties or those in areas with few transactions present challenges for AI models, potentially reducing valuation accuracy.

Challenges in Ensuring AI Valuation Reliability

- **Data Gaps and Biases:** AI models can only analyze available data, which may not capture the full picture, especially in less transparent or homogeneous markets. Additionally, historical data biases can skew AI valuations, requiring careful model design and data selection.

- **Model Overfitting and Generalization:** AI models that are overfitted to the training data may perform poorly on new or unseen data, leading to less reliable valuations. Ensuring models are well-generalized is crucial for maintaining accuracy across different properties and markets.

- **Regulatory and Ethical Considerations:** Ensuring AI valuations comply with industry standards and ethical guidelines is essential for their reliability. Models must be transparent, fair, and free from discriminatory biases.

- **Technological and Methodological Limitations:** Current technological and methodological limitations may restrict the scope of factors AI can consider, potentially overlooking elements that a human appraiser might deem significant.

Enhancing the Accuracy and Reliability of AI Valuations

- **Improving Data Collection and Management:** Implementing robust data collection, cleaning, and management practices can significantly enhance the quality of data fed into AI models, thereby improving valuation accuracy.
- **Advancing AI Models and Algorithms:** Continuously developing and refining AI models to better capture complex market dynamics and property characteristics can enhance valuation reliability.
- **Incorporating Human Expertise:** Combining AI valuations with human expertise and local market knowledge can address gaps in AI assessments, particularly for unique properties or in rapidly changing markets.
- **Regular Model Validation and Updates:** Periodically validating AI models against actual market transactions and updating them to reflect current market conditions are critical for maintaining their accuracy over time.
- **Transparency and Explainability:** Making AI models more transparent and their decisions explainable can build trust in AI valuations, allowing users to understand and verify the basis of the estimates.

Conclusion

While AI-driven valuations offer significant advantages in terms of speed and cost-efficiency, ensuring their accuracy and reliability is paramount for their effective use in real estate. By addressing the challenges and continuously improving data quality, model sophistication, and incorporating human insights, the accuracy and reliability of AI valuations can be significantly enhanced, making them a valuable tool in the real estate valuation process.

7. AI for Due Diligence in Real Estate

Due diligence is a critical phase in real estate transactions, involving thorough investigations to assess the viability, risks, and compliance of properties. The advent of Artificial Intelligence (AI) has revolutionized this process, offering tools that streamline investigations, enhance accuracy, and uncover insights that might otherwise go unnoticed. This chapter explores the integration of AI in real estate due diligence, highlighting its applications, benefits, and the transformative impact it brings to the industry.

Transforming Due Diligence with AI

AI transforms the due diligence process by automating data collection and analysis, providing predictive insights, and identifying potential risks and opportunities. Key areas where AI is making an impact include:

- **Legal Compliance and Document Analysis:** AI-powered tools can swiftly review legal documents, contracts, and regulatory filings, ensuring compliance and identifying potential legal issues. Natural Language Processing (NLP) algorithms are particularly effective in parsing complex legal language and extracting relevant information.
- **Financial Analysis:** AI systems can analyze financial records, cash flow statements, and investment returns, offering a comprehensive view of a property's financial health. Machine learning models can also predict future

financial performance based on historical data and market trends.

- **Property and Market Analysis:** AI tools assess property conditions, market position, and comparative market analysis (CMA) by analyzing vast datasets, including market reports, property listings, and transaction histories. This comprehensive analysis aids in understanding the property's value and market potential.
- **Risk Assessment:** AI algorithms evaluate various risk factors, including environmental risks, market volatility, and tenant stability. Predictive analytics can forecast potential issues, allowing investors to mitigate risks proactively.

Applications of AI in Due Diligence

AI's capabilities are leveraged across multiple due diligence domains:

- **Title and Ownership Verification:** AI streamlines the verification of property titles and ownership history, detecting any discrepancies or legal encumbrances that could affect the transaction.
- **Building Condition Assessment:** Through image recognition and analysis, AI evaluates the condition of properties, identifying areas that require repair or may pose future issues.
- **Environmental and Zoning Compliance:** AI tools analyze environmental reports and zoning regulations, ensuring that properties comply with local laws and identifying any potential environmental liabilities.

- **Tenant and Lease Analysis:** For commercial properties, AI examines tenant leases, stability, and payment histories, providing insights into the property's revenue potential and tenant risk profile.

Advantages of Leveraging AI in Due Diligence

The integration of AI in the due diligence process offers several key benefits:

- **Efficiency and Speed:** AI significantly reduces the time required for due diligence by automating routine tasks and analyses, allowing for quicker transaction closures.
- **Depth and Accuracy of Analysis:** AI's ability to process and analyze large volumes of data ensures a thorough and accurate assessment, minimizing the risk of oversight.
- **Predictive Insights:** Beyond current assessments, AI provides forecasts and predictive insights, enabling investors to make informed decisions based on future potential and risks.
- **Cost Reduction:** By streamlining the due diligence process, AI reduces the associated costs, making comprehensive investigations more accessible and affordable.

Challenges and Considerations

While AI offers substantial advantages, it also presents challenges:

- **Data Quality and Accessibility:** The effectiveness of AI in due diligence depends on the availability and quality of data, which can vary significantly across markets and regions.

- **Complexity and Black Box Algorithms:** Some AI models, especially deep learning systems, can be opaque, making it difficult to understand how conclusions are derived.
- **Integration with Traditional Processes:** Integrating AI tools with existing due diligence workflows requires careful planning and adaptation.

The Future of AI in Due Diligence

As AI technology advances, its application in due diligence is expected to become more sophisticated, with enhanced capabilities for anomaly detection, risk forecasting, and integration with blockchain for secure and transparent record-keeping. The future of AI in due diligence promises even greater efficiency, depth of analysis, and strategic insights, further transforming the real estate due diligence landscape.

Conclusion

AI has significantly enhanced the due diligence process in real estate, offering tools that automate analyses, predict outcomes, and uncover hidden risks. By embracing AI, real estate professionals can conduct more thorough, accurate, and efficient due diligence, ensuring informed decision-making and successful investments. As AI technologies continue to evolve, their role in due diligence will expand, setting new standards for thoroughness and insight in real estate transactions.

Streamlining Property Research with AI

Property research, a cornerstone of successful real estate investment, involves a meticulous examination of various factors including market trends, property specifics, legal compliance, and financial viability. The integration of Artificial Intelligence (AI) into this process is revolutionizing how investors and professionals approach property research, streamlining tasks, enhancing accuracy, and uncovering deep insights. This chapter delves into how AI is facilitating more efficient and effective property research.

Automating Data Collection and Analysis

AI excels in aggregating and analyzing vast amounts of data from diverse sources, such as property listings, public records, and market reports. Machine learning algorithms can sift through this data, identifying relevant information and trends that are crucial for comprehensive property research.

- **Market Trend Analysis:** AI models analyze historical data to identify market trends, offering insights into price movements, demand fluctuations, and investment hotspots.
- **Property Feature Extraction:** AI-powered image recognition and natural language processing (NLP) can extract detailed information from property images and descriptions, providing a thorough understanding of property features and conditions.

Enhancing Comparative Market Analysis (CMA)

Comparative Market Analysis (CMA) is a vital component of property research, involving the comparison of a subject property with similar properties in the area to assess its value. AI streamlines this process by:

- **Automating Comparables Selection:** AI algorithms can quickly identify and analyze comparable properties, considering factors like location, size, condition, and features.
- **Dynamic Pricing Models:** AI-driven models offer real-time valuation adjustments based on changing market conditions and comparables, providing more accurate and current market value estimations.

Predictive Analytics for Future Valuations

Predictive analytics, a key feature of AI in real estate, forecasts future property values and market conditions. This forward-looking approach enables investors to anticipate changes and make informed decisions.

- **Forecasting Property Values:** AI models predict future property values based on trends, economic indicators, and market dynamics.
- **Identifying Emerging Markets:** AI algorithms can spot early signs of neighborhood revitalization or emerging markets, allowing investors to capitalize on opportunities before they become mainstream.

Risk Assessment and Mitigation

AI significantly enhances the risk assessment aspect of property research by analyzing a multitude of risk factors and their potential impact on investments.

- **Market Volatility Analysis:** AI tools assess market stability and predict potential volatility, aiding in risk management.
- **Environmental and Regulatory Risk Assessment:** AI evaluates environmental risks and regulatory compliance, ensuring that investments are secure and sustainable.

Streamlining Legal and Financial Due Diligence

AI transforms the legal and financial aspects of property research by automating the analysis of legal documents and financial records.

- **Document Analysis:** NLP algorithms review contracts, leases, and regulatory documents, extracting critical information and identifying potential legal issues.
- **Financial Health Analysis:** AI systems analyze financial statements and investment returns, offering insights into a property's financial performance and viability.

Customizable Reporting and Insights

AI platforms provide customizable dashboards and reporting tools, allowing users to tailor the property research process to their specific needs and preferences.

- **Interactive Dashboards:** Users can interact with AI-generated data visualizations, exploring different aspects of property research in depth.
- **Targeted Insights:** AI tools can generate insights and recommendations based on user-defined criteria, streamlining the decision-making process.

Challenges and Future Directions

While AI significantly streamlines property research, challenges such as data privacy, model transparency, and integration with traditional processes remain. Future advancements in AI are expected to address these challenges, offering more sophisticated analytical tools and seamless integration with existing real estate workflows.

Conclusion

AI is transforming property research, offering tools that automate and enhance various aspects of the process. By leveraging AI, real estate professionals and investors can conduct more efficient, accurate, and comprehensive research, leading to informed investment decisions and successful outcomes. As AI technology continues to evolve, its role in property research is set to expand, further streamlining and enriching the real estate investment landscape.

AI in Assessing Property Conditions

Evaluating the condition of a property is a crucial step in real estate transactions, investment analysis, and portfolio management. Traditional methods rely heavily on physical inspections and subjective assessments, which can be time-consuming and potentially inconsistent. Artificial Intelligence (AI) is revolutionizing this aspect of real estate by providing tools that offer more objective, efficient, and detailed assessments of property conditions. This chapter explores the integration of AI in property condition assessment, its methodologies, applications, and the value it adds to real estate professionals and investors.

AI Technologies in Property Condition Assessment

AI leverages a variety of technologies to assess property conditions, each offering unique insights and advantages:

- **Computer Vision and Image Recognition:** AI-powered computer vision algorithms analyze property photos and videos to identify structural features, detect signs of wear and tear, and even estimate the age of various components. This technology can highlight areas that may require repair or maintenance without the need for a physical inspection.
- **Natural Language Processing (NLP):** NLP is used to extract and analyze information from property listings, inspection reports, and maintenance records. By parsing textual data, AI can identify mentions of property features, recent upgrades, or issues that may not be visible in images.
- **Predictive Analytics:** AI can predict potential future issues based on historical data, current condition assessments, and patterns identified in similar properties. This forward-looking analysis helps in proactive maintenance and risk management.

Methodologies for AI-Driven Condition Assessments

AI-driven property condition assessments typically involve the following methodologies:

1. **Data Collection:** Gathering a comprehensive set of property images, videos, and documents that provide insights into the property's condition.
2. **Feature Extraction:** Using computer vision and NLP to extract relevant information from the collected data, such as the condition of the roof, walls, flooring, and presence of features like solar panels or swimming pools.
3. **Anomaly Detection:** AI algorithms identify anomalies or deviations from normal conditions, flagging potential issues such as cracks, leaks, or structural damage.
4. **Condition Scoring:** AI models can assign condition scores to various aspects of the property, providing a quantifiable measure of its overall state and specific components.
5. **Comparative Analysis:** Comparing the subject property's condition with similar properties in the database to assess its relative condition and identify areas that may require attention.

Applications of AI in Property Condition Assessment

The use of AI in assessing property conditions finds applications across multiple real estate activities:

- **Pre-purchase Inspections:** AI tools can provide potential buyers with an initial assessment of a property's condition, helping them make informed decisions and prepare for negotiations.
- **Portfolio Management:** For real estate investors and property managers, AI-driven condition assessments offer a scalable way to monitor the health of multiple properties, prioritize maintenance, and plan renovations.
- **Insurance and Appraisals:** Insurers and appraisers can use AI assessments to determine property values more accurately and assess risks associated with property conditions.
- **Regulatory Compliance:** AI can help ensure properties meet building codes and safety regulations by identifying non-compliance issues and potential hazards.

Advantages and Challenges

AI-driven property condition assessments offer several advantages, including speed, objectivity, and scalability. However, challenges such as data privacy concerns, the need for high-quality data, and the integration of AI tools with existing workflows must be addressed. Ensuring that AI assessments complement, rather than replace, traditional inspections and expert evaluations is also crucial for their effective use.

Future Directions

As AI technology advances, future developments may include more sophisticated image recognition capabilities, integration with IoT devices for real-time condition monitoring, and augmented reality (AR) applications for virtual inspections. The continued evolution of AI in property condition assessment promises to further enhance the accuracy, efficiency, and comprehensiveness of property evaluations in the real estate industry.

Conclusion

AI is transforming the way property conditions are assessed, offering tools that automate the process, provide detailed analyses, and uncover insights that may not be apparent through traditional methods. By leveraging AI, real estate professionals and investors can achieve a deeper understanding of property conditions, leading to more informed decision-making and effective property management. As AI technologies continue to evolve, their role in property condition assessment is set to expand, further enriching the capabilities of the real estate sector.

8. Finding Off-Market Properties with AI

Discovering off-market properties—those not listed on public platforms or MLS—presents a significant opportunity for real estate investors to find unique deals before they hit the competitive open market. Artificial Intelligence (AI) is revolutionizing this aspect of real estate investment by offering innovative ways to identify and analyze such properties. This chapter explores how AI facilitates the discovery of off-market properties, the technologies involved, and the strategic advantages it provides to investors.

Leveraging AI for Off-Market Discovery

AI enables the identification of off-market properties through various advanced techniques and data sources, significantly broadening the scope of opportunities for investors:

- **Predictive Analytics:** AI algorithms analyze patterns in property transactions, ownership data, and market trends to predict which properties are likely to be sold or become available soon, even if they're not currently listed.
- **Social Media and Sentiment Analysis:** By monitoring social media platforms and online forums, AI tools can detect signals indicating a property owner's intention to sell, such as posts about relocating, financial distress, or property upgrades.
- **Public Records and Non-Traditional Data Sources:** AI sifts through public records, including tax

information, divorce records, and probate sales, to identify potential off-market opportunities. Non-traditional data sources like utility records or construction permits can also provide hints about properties that may soon enter the market.

AI Technologies Facilitating Off-Market Searches

The search for off-market properties is powered by a range of AI technologies, each contributing unique insights:

- **Natural Language Processing (NLP):** NLP algorithms analyze textual data from various sources, extracting relevant information about potential property transactions or owner intentions.
- **Machine Learning Models:** These models use historical data to learn patterns associated with off-market transactions, refining their predictions over time to identify likely off-market properties more accurately.
- **Geospatial Analysis:** By analyzing geographical data, AI can identify properties in high-demand areas or those undergoing significant changes, which might indicate potential off-market opportunities.
- **Data Aggregation and Integration:** AI platforms aggregate data from multiple sources, providing a comprehensive view that can reveal off-market properties that might be overlooked by traditional search methods.

Applications and Strategies

Investors leverage AI to uncover off-market properties in various ways, each tailored to specific investment strategies:

- **Direct Outreach Campaigns:** Armed with AI-generated insights, investors can target potential off-market properties with personalized outreach campaigns, offering to buy directly from owners.
- **Portfolio Expansion:** For investors looking to expand their portfolios in specific markets or property types, AI can identify off-market opportunities that align with their investment criteria.
- **Wholesaling and Flipping:** Real estate wholesalers and flippers use AI to find off-market deals they can acquire below market value and either sell to other investors or renovate and sell at a profit.

Advantages of AI in Off-Market Searches

The use of AI in finding off-market properties offers several advantages:

- **Competitive Edge:** Discovering off-market properties gives investors a head start before these properties become widely known, reducing competition and potentially leading to better deal terms.
- **Efficiency:** AI automates the labor-intensive process of identifying potential off-market deals, saving time and resources.
- **Data-Driven Decisions:** The insights provided by AI are grounded in data, enabling more informed investment decisions and risk assessment.

Challenges and Ethical Considerations

While AI offers powerful tools for off-market searches, investors face challenges such as ensuring data accuracy, respecting privacy laws, and navigating the ethical implications of using personal information for investment purposes.

The Future of AI in Off-Market Property Searches

As AI technology advances, its capabilities in identifying off-market properties will become even more sophisticated, with improved accuracy, broader data integration, and enhanced predictive analytics. The future may also see more collaborative AI platforms that connect property owners directly with investors, further streamlining off-market transactions.

Conclusion

AI is transforming the landscape of off-market property searches, offering real estate investors innovative tools to discover unique investment opportunities. By harnessing the power of AI, investors can navigate the competitive real estate market more effectively, uncovering hidden gems and securing deals with significant potential. As AI technologies continue to evolve, their impact on off-market property searches is set to grow, offering even greater advantages to savvy investors.

Techniques for Uncovering Hidden Gems in Real Estate

In the competitive world of real estate investment, finding hidden gems—properties with untapped potential or undervalued assets—can lead to significant returns. Beyond the traditional methods, several innovative techniques, enhanced by the latest technologies, can help investors uncover these elusive opportunities. This chapter explores a range of strategies for identifying hidden gems in the real estate market, from leveraging data analytics to engaging with local communities.

Data-Driven Market Analysis

Utilizing comprehensive data analytics is key to identifying undervalued properties or emerging markets. Advanced software and platforms can analyze vast amounts of data to pinpoint areas with growth potential or properties priced below market value due to various factors.

- **Predictive Analytics:** Use AI and machine learning to forecast market trends, property value appreciation, and neighborhood development, highlighting areas ripe for investment.
- **Comparative Market Analysis (CMA):** Employ automated tools to conduct extensive CMAs, identifying properties that are undervalued compared to similar listings in the area.

Geographic Information Systems (GIS)

GIS technology offers a spatial perspective on real estate opportunities, integrating various data layers to reveal insights not apparent through traditional analysis.

- **Location Analytics:** Analyze proximity to amenities, infrastructure developments, and transportation links to assess the potential impact on property values.

- **Demographic and Economic Trends:** Overlay demographic information and economic indicators to identify areas undergoing positive transformations.

Social Media and Online Platforms

Social media platforms and online forums can be goldmines for discovering off-market deals or properties that haven't yet caught the mainstream attention.

- **Sentiment Analysis:** Use NLP tools to gauge public sentiment and emerging trends in specific neighborhoods or property types.
- **Community Engagement:** Participate in local online forums and social media groups to get insights from residents and property owners about up-and-coming areas or potential sales.

Networking and Community Engagement

Building strong relationships with local communities, real estate professionals, and industry groups can lead to valuable tips on hidden gems.

- **Local Events and Meetups:** Attend community events, real estate meetups, and seminars to connect with insiders who have firsthand knowledge of the area.
- **Partnerships with Local Businesses:** Engage with local businesses and contractors who might have insights into properties with potential or upcoming developments.

Technology-Enhanced Property Scouting

Leveraging technology can significantly enhance traditional property scouting methods, providing a competitive edge in finding hidden gems.

- **Drones and Aerial Photography:** Use drones for aerial surveys of properties and neighborhoods, revealing insights such as lot sizes, property conditions, and surrounding developments.
- **Virtual Tours and Augmented Reality:** Utilize virtual tour software and AR apps to explore properties remotely, identifying features or potential that might not be listed in traditional property descriptions.

Specialized Investment Niches

Focusing on less conventional property types or investment strategies can uncover opportunities that others might overlook.

- **Distressed Properties:** Look for properties in foreclosure, bank-owned assets, or those in need of significant renovation as potential hidden gems.
- **Niche Markets:** Explore niche markets like historic homes, eco-friendly properties, or live-work spaces that might offer unique investment opportunities.

Regulatory Changes and Zoning Analysis

Stay informed about local regulatory changes, zoning updates, and urban planning initiatives that could affect property values and investment potential.

- **Zoning Changes:** Monitor local government discussions and plans for zoning changes that could enhance property usability and value.
- **Incentive Programs:** Look for government or local incentives for redevelopment, historic preservation, or green building that could add value to properties.

Continuous Learning and Adaptation

The real estate market is constantly evolving, and staying informed about the latest trends, technologies, and investment strategies is crucial for finding hidden gems.

- **Industry Publications and Reports:** Regularly review real estate publications, market reports, and investment analyses to stay ahead of market trends.
- **Educational Resources:** Participate in webinars, courses, and workshops focusing on innovative real estate investment strategies and technologies.

Conclusion

Uncovering hidden gems in real estate requires a combination of traditional diligence, innovative technology, and a deep understanding of market dynamics. By employing a diverse set of techniques—from data-driven analytics to community engagement and leveraging the latest in technology—investors can enhance their ability to discover properties with significant untapped potential. As the real estate landscape continues to evolve, staying adaptable, informed, and connected will be key to capitalizing on these hidden opportunities.

Success Stories: AI and Off-Market Deals

The integration of Artificial Intelligence (AI) in the real estate sector has led to numerous success stories, particularly in uncovering and capitalizing on off-market deals. These narratives not only highlight the potential of AI in transforming investment strategies but also serve as a testament to the innovative approaches adopted by investors and real estate professionals. This chapter delves into a selection of success stories that showcase the effective use of AI in identifying and securing off-market real estate opportunities.

Case Study 1: Urban Revitalization Project

Background: A real estate development company aimed to identify undervalued properties in urban areas slated for revitalization.

AI Application: The company utilized AI-driven predictive analytics to analyze historical data, urban development plans, and social media sentiment. The AI model identified potential off-market properties in neighborhoods on the cusp of significant transformation due to upcoming infrastructure projects and increasing cultural activities.

Outcome: By acquiring several off-market properties early in the revitalization phase, the company was able to secure them at below-market prices. These investments yielded substantial returns as the area's popularity and property values surged following the completion of the development projects.

Case Study 2: Portfolio Expansion in Emerging Markets

Background: An investment firm sought to expand its portfolio by targeting off-market residential properties in emerging markets with high growth potential.

AI Application: Leveraging geospatial analysis and machine learning, the firm's AI platform assessed various emerging markets for signs of growth, such as increased economic activity, demographic shifts, and housing demand. The platform identified properties owned by distressed sellers or those not yet listed for sale.

Outcome: The firm successfully acquired a series of off-market properties in these identified markets, capitalizing on lower acquisition costs. The strategic expansion significantly enhanced the firm's portfolio diversity and returns as the markets matured.

Case Study 3: High-End Property Acquisition

Background: A luxury real estate agency aimed to provide exclusive off-market listings to high-net-worth clients seeking unique properties.

AI Application: The agency used an AI tool equipped with NLP to monitor high-end property forums, social networks, and owner signals indicating a willingness to sell privately. The tool also analyzed property features and market trends to assess the uniqueness and potential value of these off-market listings.

Outcome: The agency was able to offer its clients an exclusive selection of high-end off-market properties, meeting their unique preferences and ensuring privacy in transactions. This strategy significantly enhanced client satisfaction and loyalty, positioning the agency as a leader in the luxury real estate market.

Case Study 4: Distressed Property Investments

Background: A real estate investor specialized in renovating and flipping distressed properties sought new opportunities for investment.

AI Application: Using an AI system, the investor analyzed public records, including foreclosure notices, tax delinquencies, and utility shutoffs, to identify distressed properties that were not yet on the market. The system prioritized properties based on estimated repair costs and potential market value post-renovation.

Outcome: The investor was able to purchase several distressed properties before they were listed, at prices well below market value. After renovation, these properties were sold at a significant profit, demonstrating the effectiveness of AI in identifying lucrative off-market opportunities.

Conclusion

These success stories illustrate the diverse applications and significant advantages of leveraging AI in the search for off-market real estate deals. By utilizing advanced analytics, predictive modeling, and data aggregation, investors and professionals can uncover hidden opportunities, gain a competitive edge, and achieve remarkable success in the real estate market. As AI technology continues to evolve, its role in identifying and securing off-market deals is expected to grow, offering even more innovative avenues for real estate investment and development.

9. The Future of AI in Deal-Finding

As Artificial Intelligence (AI) continues to evolve and integrate into various sectors, its impact on real estate deal-finding is poised for significant expansion. The future of AI in real estate promises enhanced capabilities, broader applications, and innovative approaches to identifying and securing lucrative investment opportunities. This chapter explores the emerging trends, potential advancements, and the transformative potential of AI in revolutionizing deal-finding in the real estate sector.

Advancements in AI Technologies

The continuous development of AI technologies will drive the future of deal-finding, with several key areas of advancement:

- **Improved Predictive Analytics:** Future AI systems will offer even more sophisticated predictive models, leveraging larger datasets and more complex algorithms to forecast market trends, property values, and investment opportunities with greater accuracy.
- **Enhanced Natural Language Processing (NLP):** NLP will become more nuanced, allowing AI to better understand and analyze human language. This will enable more effective sentiment analysis, deeper insights from unstructured data, and more personalized interactions with investors.
- **Augmented and Virtual Reality Integration:** AR and VR technologies will increasingly integrate with AI to

provide immersive property tours, detailed condition assessments, and virtual staging, enhancing the deal-evaluation process.

- **Blockchain and AI Synergy:** The integration of blockchain technology with AI will enhance transparency, security, and efficiency in transactions, making the deal-finding process more trustworthy and streamlined.

Expanding Applications of AI in Real Estate

AI's applications in real estate deal-finding will broaden, encompassing new areas and offering innovative solutions:

- **Automated Investment Portfolios:** AI will tailor investment portfolios to individual investor preferences and goals, automatically identifying and suggesting deals that fit specified criteria.
- **Smart Contracting and Transactions:** AI will play a crucial role in smart contracts, automating and optimizing contract terms based on real-time market data and individual deal parameters.
- **Urban Development and Planning:** AI will contribute to urban planning and development projects, identifying optimal locations for development based on predictive modeling of urban growth and demographic shifts.
- **Sustainable Investing:** AI will facilitate the identification of eco-friendly and sustainable investment opportunities, aligning with growing trends towards green building and sustainable development.

Overcoming Challenges

As AI advances, addressing challenges and ethical considerations will be paramount to ensure its positive impact on deal-finding:

- **Data Privacy and Security:** Ensuring the ethical use of data and protecting investor privacy will be crucial as AI systems handle increasingly sensitive information.
- **Bias and Fairness:** AI systems must be designed to avoid biases in deal recommendations and valuations, ensuring fairness and objectivity in investment opportunities.
- **Regulatory Compliance:** AI applications in real estate must navigate a complex regulatory landscape, adapting to legal standards across different markets and jurisdictions.

The Human-AI Partnership

The future of AI in deal-finding will not render human insight obsolete but will instead foster a synergistic relationship between AI and real estate professionals:

- **Complementary Expertise:** AI will augment human expertise, providing data-driven insights and efficiency gains, while human professionals will offer contextual understanding and strategic decision-making.
- **Collaborative Platforms:** Emerging platforms will facilitate collaboration between AI systems and real estate professionals, enhancing communication, decision-making, and transaction processes.

- **Continuous Learning and Adaptation:** AI systems will learn from human feedback and market outcomes, continuously improving their recommendations and strategies.

Conclusion

The future of AI in deal-finding in real estate is bright, with advancements in technology, expanding applications, and the potential for transformative impacts on the industry. By embracing AI, real estate professionals and investors can look forward to more efficient, informed, and strategic deal-finding processes. As AI technologies evolve, staying informed and adaptable will be key to leveraging their full potential in the dynamic landscape of real estate investment.

Upcoming Trends in AI and Real Estate

The intersection of Artificial Intelligence (AI) and real estate is an area of rapid evolution and innovation. As AI technologies advance, they bring forth new trends that are set to redefine the real estate landscape, offering unprecedented opportunities and efficiencies. This section explores the most promising upcoming trends in AI within the real estate sector, highlighting how they may shape the future of property investment, management, and transaction processes.

1. AI-Driven Smart Cities and Urban Planning

AI is playing a pivotal role in the development of smart cities, where urban planning and real estate development are optimized through data analytics and machine learning. AI algorithms analyze vast amounts of data related to traffic patterns, energy usage, and environmental factors, facilitating the design of more efficient, sustainable, and livable urban spaces. This trend not only impacts real estate development projects but also influences investment decisions by highlighting areas with high growth potential.

2. Enhanced Property Management with IoT Integration

The integration of AI with the Internet of Things (IoT) is revolutionizing property management. Smart buildings equipped with IoT sensors generate real-time data on energy consumption, occupancy patterns, and maintenance needs. AI algorithms process this data to optimize building operations, reduce energy costs, and improve tenant experiences. This trend is set to become more prevalent, offering property managers and investors insights that drive operational efficiencies and enhance property values.

3. Blockchain-Enabled Transaction Platforms

Blockchain technology, combined with AI, is set to transform real estate transactions by enhancing transparency, security, and efficiency. Smart contracts, powered by blockchain, automate transaction processes based on predefined conditions verified by AI. This trend is expected to reduce the need for intermediaries, streamline transactions, and minimize fraud, making the buying, selling, and leasing processes more straightforward and trustworthy.

4. Virtual Reality (VR) and Augmented Reality (AR) in Property Showcasing

AI-enhanced VR and AR applications are changing the way properties are marketed and viewed. Potential buyers and tenants can take virtual tours of properties, customized in real-time through AI to suit their preferences. This immersive experience allows for a more interactive and engaging property showcasing, enabling buyers to make more informed decisions without the need for physical visits. This trend is likely to grow, particularly in the luxury real estate market and in situations where remote viewing is preferred.

5. Predictive Analytics for Personalized Investment Opportunities

AI's predictive analytics capabilities are becoming more sophisticated, offering investors personalized property recommendations based on their investment history, preferences, and market trends. These AI systems analyze large datasets to identify opportunities that match investor profiles, optimizing investment portfolios and maximizing returns. This trend promises to make investment processes more targeted and efficient.

6. AI in Construction and Development

AI is set to play a more significant role in the construction and development phase of real estate. From optimizing project designs through generative design algorithms to monitoring construction progress and managing project risks with predictive analytics, AI applications in construction are enhancing efficiency, reducing costs, and improving safety. This trend is expected to accelerate, driven by the need for more sustainable and efficient construction practices.

7. Automated Valuations and Appraisals

The accuracy and efficiency of property valuations and appraisals are being enhanced through AI-driven models. These Automated Valuation Models (AVMs) leverage vast amounts of market and property data to provide instant, accurate property valuations. As these models become more advanced, they are expected to become a standard tool in the real estate industry, used by investors, lenders, and appraisers alike.

Conclusion

The upcoming trends in AI and real estate signify a transformative period ahead for the industry. From the way properties are designed, managed, and transacted, to how investments are made and portfolios are managed, AI is at the forefront of innovation. As these trends unfold, staying informed and adaptable will be crucial for real estate professionals and investors aiming to leverage the full potential of AI in this dynamic landscape.

What Next for Investors in the AI-Enhanced Real Estate Landscape?

As the real estate landscape continues to be reshaped by advancements in Artificial Intelligence (AI), investors are poised at the brink of a new era filled with opportunities and challenges. The integration of AI into various facets of real estate, from deal-finding and property valuation to portfolio management and transaction processes, necessitates a strategic reevaluation of investment approaches. Here's what's next for investors navigating this AI-enhanced real estate landscape:

Embrace Continuous Learning

The rapid pace of technological advancements in AI and real estate requires investors to commit to continuous learning. Staying abreast of the latest AI tools, platforms, and methodologies will be crucial for leveraging technology effectively. Investors should seek educational resources, attend industry conferences, and participate in professional networks focused on the intersection of AI and real estate.

Leverage AI for Data-Driven Decisions

AI's ability to analyze vast amounts of data offers investors unprecedented insights into market trends, property valuations, and investment risks. Embracing AI tools for predictive analytics, market analysis, and property research will enable investors to make more informed, data-driven decisions, reducing reliance on intuition and conventional wisdom.

Diversify Investment Strategies

The AI-enhanced real estate landscape presents a diverse array of investment opportunities, from traditional residential and commercial properties to emerging niches like smart buildings and sustainable developments. Investors should consider diversifying their portfolios to include a mix of traditional and innovative assets, leveraging AI to identify and evaluate potential investments across various segments.

Adopt a Proactive Approach to Innovation

Investors should adopt a proactive stance towards technological innovation, exploring new AI applications and platforms that can offer competitive advantages. This may involve investing in AI startups, partnering with technology providers, or developing in-house AI capabilities to stay ahead in the rapidly evolving market.

Prioritize Ethical and Responsible Investing

As AI brings greater efficiency and insight, it also raises ethical considerations, particularly regarding data privacy, security, and bias. Investors must prioritize ethical and responsible investing practices, ensuring that AI applications comply with legal standards and ethical norms. This commitment to ethical investing will not only mitigate risks but also enhance reputation and investor trust.

Enhance Collaboration with AI Experts

The complexity of AI technologies necessitates collaboration between real estate professionals and AI experts. Investors should consider building or joining multidisciplinary teams that combine real estate acumen with AI expertise, fostering an environment where technology and domain knowledge intersect to create value.

Prepare for Regulatory Evolution

The legal and regulatory landscape surrounding AI in real estate is evolving. Investors must stay informed about regulatory changes, participate in industry dialogues, and advocate for policies that support innovation while protecting stakeholders' interests. Being proactive in regulatory preparedness will ensure compliance and mitigate potential legal risks.

Focus on Sustainable and Smart Investments

AI's role in promoting sustainability and smart development in real estate is growing. Investors should focus on properties and projects that leverage AI for energy efficiency, environmental sustainability, and smart infrastructure, aligning investment strategies with global sustainability goals.

Conclusion

For real estate investors, the future in an AI-enhanced landscape is bright with possibilities. By embracing AI, focusing on continuous learning, and adopting ethical, diversified, and innovative investment strategies, investors can navigate the complexities of the modern real estate market. The journey ahead will require adaptability, foresight, and a commitment to leveraging technology for sustainable, profitable, and responsible real estate investment

10. Implementing AI in Your Investment Strategy

Incorporating Artificial Intelligence (AI) into real estate investment strategies is no longer a futuristic concept but a practical approach to gaining a competitive edge in today's market. AI's ability to analyze vast datasets, predict market trends, and identify lucrative opportunities can significantly enhance investment decisions and outcomes. This chapter provides a comprehensive guide on integrating AI into your real estate investment strategy, ensuring you harness the full potential of this transformative technology.

Understanding the AI Landscape in Real Estate

Before integrating AI into your investment strategy, it's crucial to understand the spectrum of AI tools and applications available in the real estate sector. From predictive analytics and automated valuation models (AVMs) to AI-driven property management systems and virtual assistant technologies, familiarizing yourself with these tools will help you identify the ones most relevant to your investment goals.

Setting Clear Objectives

Define clear, measurable objectives for incorporating AI into your investment strategy. Whether it's improving the accuracy of property valuations, identifying off-market deals, optimizing your portfolio, or enhancing operational efficiencies, having specific goals will guide your AI integration efforts and help measure success.

Assessing Your Current Capabilities

Evaluate your current investment processes and technological infrastructure to identify areas where AI can offer the most significant improvements. This assessment should consider your data collection and management practices, analytical capabilities, and the scalability of your current systems.

Choosing the Right AI Tools and Partners

Select AI tools and platforms that align with your investment objectives and operational needs. Consider factors such as ease of use, integration with existing systems, scalability, and the level of customer support provided. In some cases, partnering with AI service providers or proptech startups can offer access to advanced technologies and expertise.

Investing in Data Quality and Management

The effectiveness of AI in real estate hinges on the quality and comprehensiveness of the underlying data. Invest in robust data collection, cleaning, and management practices to ensure your AI tools have access to accurate, current, and relevant data. This may involve enhancing your data infrastructure, adopting standardized data formats, and establishing data governance policies.

Building or Enhancing Your Team's AI Literacy

Ensure your team has the necessary skills and knowledge to work effectively with AI tools. This may involve training existing staff, hiring new talent with AI expertise, or both.

Fostering a culture of continuous learning and innovation will be crucial for adapting to the rapidly evolving AI landscape.

Implementing AI Tools with a Phased Approach

Adopt a phased approach to implementing AI in your investment strategy, starting with pilot projects or specific aspects of your operations. This allows you to gauge the effectiveness of AI tools, make necessary adjustments, and build organizational buy-in before wider deployment.

Monitoring Performance and Adapting Your Strategy

Continuously monitor the performance of AI tools against your investment objectives, using metrics and key performance indicators (KPIs) to assess their impact. Be prepared to adapt your strategy based on performance data, feedback from your team, and evolving market conditions.

Staying Informed and Adaptable

The AI and real estate landscapes are continuously evolving. Stay informed about the latest developments in AI technologies, real estate market trends, and regulatory changes. Being adaptable and open to new ideas and technologies will be key to maximizing the benefits of AI in your investment strategy.

Conclusion

Integrating AI into your real estate investment strategy offers significant advantages, from enhanced decision-making and operational efficiencies to competitive differentiation. By understanding the AI landscape, setting clear objectives, investing in data quality, and adopting a phased implementation approach, you can effectively harness the power of AI to achieve your investment goals. As the real estate sector continues to embrace technological innovation, being at the forefront of AI integration will position you for success in the dynamic and competitive world of real estate investing.

Getting Started with AI Tools in Real Estate

Embracing Artificial Intelligence (AI) in real estate can seem daunting, but it's increasingly becoming a necessity for staying competitive and making informed decisions. Whether you're an investor, agent, or property manager, starting with AI tools can streamline operations, enhance decision-making, and uncover new opportunities. Here's a practical guide to getting started with AI in real estate.

Step 1: Identify Your Needs and Goals

Begin by defining what you want to achieve with AI. Are you looking to improve property valuations, optimize your property search, enhance customer service, or predict market trends? Clear objectives will guide your choice of AI tools and measure their impact.

Step 2: Educate Yourself on AI Capabilities

Gain a basic understanding of AI and its applications in real estate. This doesn't mean becoming an AI expert but understanding what AI can do, the types of problems it can solve, and its limitations. Online courses, webinars, and industry reports can be valuable resources.

Step 3: Assess Your Data Infrastructure

AI's effectiveness heavily relies on data. Evaluate your current data collection, storage, and management practices. Ensure you have access to reliable, high-quality data, and consider investing in data infrastructure improvements if necessary.

Step 4: Explore AI Tools and Platforms

Research AI tools that align with your goals. Look for platforms specifically designed for real estate, such as those offering market analysis, property valuation, or customer relationship management with AI capabilities. Start with tools that offer trial periods or demos to get a hands-on feel without significant upfront investment.

Step 5: Start Small with Pilot Projects

Implement AI tools on a small scale initially. Choose a specific aspect of your operations where AI can have an immediate impact. Pilot projects allow you to assess the tool's effectiveness, understand its integration with your existing systems, and gauge the learning curve for your team.

Step 6: Train Your Team

Ensure your team is prepared to use AI tools effectively. This may involve formal training sessions, workshops, or self-learning modules provided by AI tool vendors. Highlight how

AI can make their work more efficient and support them through the transition.

Step 7: Monitor Results and Gather Feedback

Track the performance of AI tools against your predefined goals. Use metrics relevant to your objectives, such as time saved in property searches, improvement in lead generation, or accuracy in property valuations. Collect feedback from your team on usability, efficiency, and areas for improvement.

Step 8: Scale Up Gradually

Based on the results and feedback from pilot projects, gradually expand the use of AI tools across other areas of your operations. Scaling up should be a deliberate process, ensuring each step adds value and aligns with your overall business strategy.

Step 9: Stay Updated and Iterate

AI in real estate is a rapidly evolving field. Stay informed about new tools, updates to existing platforms, and emerging best practices. Be prepared to iterate on your AI strategy, incorporating new technologies and insights as they become available.

Step 10: Ensure Compliance and Ethical Use

As you integrate AI into your operations, be mindful of regulatory compliance, data privacy, and ethical considerations. Use AI tools responsibly, ensuring they respect user privacy and adhere to industry regulations.

Conclusion

Getting started with AI in real estate is a journey that involves setting clear goals, understanding AI capabilities, starting small, and gradually scaling up. By following these steps, you can effectively integrate AI tools into your real estate operations, unlocking new efficiencies, insights, and opportunities. Remember, the key to success with AI is continuous learning, adaptation, and a commitment to leveraging technology responsibly and ethically.

Best Practices for AI Integration in Real Estate

Integrating Artificial Intelligence (AI) into real estate operations can significantly enhance efficiency, accuracy, and decision-making. However, successful AI integration requires a strategic approach that aligns with your business objectives, operational needs, and industry standards. Here are the best practices for seamlessly incorporating AI into your real estate processes:

1. Define Clear Objectives

Before integrating AI, clearly define what you aim to achieve. Whether it's enhancing property valuations, streamlining property searches, improving customer service, or identifying investment opportunities, having specific goals will guide your AI strategy and implementation.

2. Start with a Needs Assessment

Evaluate your current processes to identify areas where AI can add the most value. Consider pain points, inefficiencies, or data-intensive tasks that could benefit from automation and advanced analytics. This assessment will help you prioritize AI integration efforts.

3. Foster Data Literacy and AI Awareness

Ensure your team understands the basics of AI and the importance of data quality and management. Conduct training sessions or workshops to build data literacy and AI awareness, emphasizing how these technologies can enhance their roles and the overall business.

4. Prioritize Data Infrastructure

AI's effectiveness hinges on the quality, accessibility, and integrity of your data. Invest in robust data collection, storage, and management systems. Ensure your data is clean, well-organized, and compliant with privacy regulations.

5. Select the Right AI Solutions

Choose AI tools and platforms that align with your objectives and integrate seamlessly with your existing systems. Consider user-friendliness, scalability, support services, and the vendor's track record in the real estate industry.

6. Implement Incrementally

Adopt a phased approach to AI integration. Start with pilot projects or specific aspects of your operations to test and refine the use of AI tools. This approach allows you to manage risks, gather insights, and build confidence in the technology.

7. Monitor Performance and Gather Feedback

Regularly assess the performance of AI tools against your objectives, using key performance indicators (KPIs) relevant to your goals. Collect feedback from users to understand their experiences, challenges, and suggestions for improvement.

8. Encourage Collaboration and Communication

Foster a collaborative environment where team members can share insights, experiences, and best practices for using AI tools. Open communication channels encourage the exchange of ideas and collective problem-solving.

9. Stay Informed and Adaptable

The AI landscape is continually evolving, with new technologies, applications, and regulatory considerations emerging regularly. Stay informed about the latest developments in AI and real estate, and be prepared to adapt your strategies and tools as needed.

10. Address Ethical and Compliance Considerations

Ensure that your use of AI adheres to ethical standards and regulatory requirements. Be transparent about how AI is used in your operations, particularly regarding data collection and analysis, and maintain a commitment to fairness and privacy.

Conclusion

Integrating AI into real estate operations offers significant benefits, from enhanced analytical capabilities to improved operational efficiencies. By following these best practices, you can ensure a smooth and successful integration of AI into your business, positioning your organization to leverage the transformative potential of AI in the real estate sector.

11. Conclusion: Navigating the Future of Real Estate with AI

As we reach the conclusion of this exploration into the integration of Artificial Intelligence (AI) in real estate, it's clear that the landscape of property investment, management, and transactions is undergoing a profound transformation. AI is not just a tool of convenience but a pivotal force driving efficiency, precision, and innovation in the real estate sector. From predictive analytics enhancing property valuations to machine learning algorithms uncovering off-market deals, AI's potential to revolutionize real estate processes is immense.

The journey towards AI integration is marked by continuous learning, strategic implementation, and adaptability to evolving technologies and market dynamics. Real estate professionals and investors equipped with AI tools and a deep understanding of their applications stand at the forefront of this new era, ready to capitalize on opportunities and navigate challenges with unprecedented insight and agility.

AI Tools for Real Estate Investors

To harness the full potential of AI in real estate, investors can leverage a variety of tools designed to streamline deal-finding and enhance investment strategies. Here's a list of notable AI tools and brief guidance on using them to find real estate deals:

1. **Zillow Zestimate**

- o **Use**: Provides instant property valuations using AI algorithms.
- o **How to Use**: Enter a property address on Zillow's platform to receive an estimated market value, aiding in quick investment analysis.

2. **Redfin Estimate**
   - o **Use**: Offers AI-driven property valuations with market comparisons.
   - o **How to Use**: Search for properties on Redfin to view estimated values and detailed market insights, helping identify undervalued properties.

3. **Roofstock**
   - o **Use**: An online marketplace for buying and selling rental properties, using AI to analyze rental yields and market conditions.
   - o **How to Use**: Browse investment properties on Roofstock, utilizing AI insights for making informed decisions on rental investments.

4. **Reonomy**
   - o **Use**: Provides AI-powered data analytics for commercial real estate, offering insights on transactions, ownership, and property details.
   - o **How to Use**: Access detailed property analyses on Reonomy to identify commercial investment opportunities and understand market trends.

5. **DealMachine**
   - o **Use**: Combines AI with direct marketing tools to identify and engage owners of potential off-market deals.
   - o **How to Use**: Use DealMachine to pinpoint properties of interest, gather owner information via AI, and initiate direct outreach campaigns.

6. **PropStream**
   - ○ **Use**: Offers comprehensive real estate data and AI-driven analytics for market analysis and lead generation.
   - ○ **How to Use**: Leverage PropStream to filter and analyze properties based on specific investment criteria, utilizing AI insights for strategic decision-making.

Final Thoughts

The integration of AI in real estate is an ongoing journey, with new developments and applications continuously emerging. By embracing AI, real estate investors and professionals can navigate the complexities of the market with greater confidence, making data-driven decisions that lead to successful outcomes. As we look to the future, the synergy between AI and real estate promises not only to enhance current practices but also to open new horizons of opportunity and innovation in the industry.

THE FUTURE OF REAL ESTATE IS HERE!

How robots are transforming the way we buy and sell homes.

Don't miss out. #robotrealestate

Recap of Key Insights from "Navigating the Future of Real Estate with AI"

In "Navigating the Future of Real Estate with AI," we embark on a journey through the transformative landscape of real estate in the age of Artificial Intelligence. This book provides a comprehensive overview of how AI is reshaping every facet of the industry, from deal discovery to property valuation and portfolio management. Key insights include:

1. **The AI Revolution in Real Estate**: Explore how AI is unlocking new levels of efficiency, accuracy, and opportunity, fundamentally changing how real estate professionals operate.
2. **Strategies for AI Integration**: Delve into practical strategies for incorporating AI into your real estate practices, ensuring a seamless transition and maximum impact.
3. **Innovative Tools and Applications**: Discover the most impactful AI tools reshaping the market, offering insights on how to leverage these technologies for competitive advantage.
4. **Uncovering Off-Market Opportunities**: Learn the secrets to finding hidden gems in the real estate market using advanced AI techniques and data analysis.
5. **The Future of AI-Driven Real Estate**: Peek into the future, examining upcoming trends and innovations that promise to further revolutionize the industry.
6. **Best Practices for Success**: Gain valuable knowledge on best practices for integrating AI into your investment strategy, enhancing decision-making and operational efficiency.

7. **Ethical Considerations and Challenges**: Navigate the ethical implications and challenges of AI in real estate, ensuring responsible and equitable use of technology.

This book is an essential guide for real estate professionals, investors, and enthusiasts looking to understand and capitalize on the power of AI. It offers a roadmap for navigating the complexities of the market with greater foresight, agility, and strategic acumen in the AI era.

Moving Forward with AI in Real Estate

As we look towards the future of real estate in the context of rapidly advancing Artificial Intelligence (AI), it's clear that embracing AI is not just an option but a necessity for professionals who wish to stay at the forefront of the industry. Moving forward with AI in real estate involves a strategic approach that acknowledges the transformative potential of technology while addressing the challenges and ethical considerations it presents. Here are key points to consider as we navigate the future of real estate with AI:

Embracing Change and Innovation

Adopt a Forward-Thinking Mindset: Stay open to new technologies and methodologies that AI brings to the real estate sector. Embracing change will be crucial for leveraging AI to its full potential.

Innovate Responsibly: While pursuing innovation, ensure that it's done responsibly, with attention to ethical considerations, data privacy, and the impact on communities and the environment.

Integrating AI Strategically

Strategic Implementation: Integrate AI into your operations strategically, focusing on areas where it can provide the most significant benefits, such as market analysis, property valuation, and customer engagement.

Skill Development: Invest in training and development to build AI literacy within your team, ensuring that your organization can effectively utilize AI tools and interpret their outputs.

Leveraging Data Effectively

Data as a Foundation: Recognize the critical role of data in AI applications. Prioritize the collection, management, and analysis of high-quality data to feed into AI systems.

Data Ethics: Maintain high standards for data ethics, ensuring that data is used in a manner that respects privacy and complies with regulations.

Fostering Collaboration

Collaborate Across Disciplines: AI in real estate benefits from interdisciplinary collaboration, bringing together experts in technology, real estate, data science, and ethics to drive innovation.

Engage with the Community: Engage with the broader real estate community, including professional associations, academic institutions, and tech startups, to share knowledge and best practices.

Staying Informed and Adaptable

Continuous Learning: The AI and real estate landscapes are continuously evolving. Commit to lifelong learning to stay informed about the latest developments, trends, and regulatory changes.

Adaptability: Be prepared to adapt your strategies and operations in response to new AI advancements and shifting market dynamics.

Navigating Ethical and Regulatory Terrain

Ethical AI Use: Ensure that AI applications in your operations adhere to ethical guidelines, focusing on fairness, transparency, and accountability.

Regulatory Compliance: Stay abreast of regulations governing AI and real estate, ensuring that your practices comply with current laws and anticipating future regulatory developments.

Looking to the Future

Anticipate Emerging Trends: Keep an eye on emerging trends at the intersection of AI and real estate, such as the rise of smart cities, blockchain integration, and the growing importance of sustainability.

Be a Thought Leader: Position yourself and your organization as thought leaders in AI-driven real estate by contributing to industry discussions, research, and innovation.

Conclusion

The journey of integrating AI into real estate is an ongoing process that offers immense potential for transformation and growth. By embracing change, leveraging data, fostering collaboration, and navigating the ethical and regulatory landscape with care, real estate professionals can harness the power of AI to drive success in an increasingly digital and data-driven world. Moving forward with AI, the real estate sector can look forward to enhanced efficiency, deeper insights, and more personalized services, shaping a future where technology and human expertise converge to create unparalleled value.

Preview of "The GPT-4 Advantage: Unlocking the Secrets of AI-Driven Income"

In an era where Artificial Intelligence is not just a buzzword but a fundamental driver of innovation, "The GPT-4 Advantage" serves as your essential guide to understanding and leveraging the latest AI technologies for income generation. This book delves into the intricacies of GPT-4, the cutting-edge AI model developed by OpenAI, revealing how entrepreneurs, businesses, and individuals can harness its capabilities to create new opportunities and streamline existing income streams.

What You'll Discover:

- **Foundational Knowledge**: Begin with a clear, accessible introduction to GPT-4, understanding its development, capabilities, and place in the broader AI landscape.

- **Practical Applications**: Explore a wide array of practical applications for GPT-4 across various industries, from content creation and digital marketing to finance and e-commerce.
- **Innovative Strategies**: Uncover innovative strategies for integrating GPT-4 into your business operations, enhancing productivity, creativity, and competitive advantage.
- **Real-World Success Stories**: Be inspired by success stories from early adopters who have effectively utilized GPT-4 to drive growth and profitability.
- **Ethical Considerations and Best Practices**: Navigate the ethical use of AI, ensuring responsible and sustainable implementation of GPT-4 in your income-generating activities.

Your Path to AI-Driven Success:

"The GPT-4 Advantage" is more than just a book; it's a roadmap to the future of AI-driven income. Whether you're looking to revolutionize your business, kickstart a new venture, or simply stay ahead in the fast-evolving digital landscape, this book provides the insights and guidance you need to succeed.

Unlock the secrets of AI-driven income with "The GPT-4 Advantage" and embark on a journey to innovation, efficiency, and unparalleled success. Available now on Amazon: The GPT-4 Advantage: Unlocking the Secrets of AI-Driven Income.

THE GPT-4
ADVANTAGE

UNLOCKING THE SECRETS OF AI-DRIVEN INCOME

ERNIE BRAVEBOY

www.ingramcontent.com/pod-product-compliance
Lightning Source LLC
Chambersburg PA
CBHW070927290526
45795CB00001B/456